imagination series # 11

ORDERING THE STORM:

How to Put Together a Book of Poems

edited by Susan Grimm

Cleveland State University Poetry Center

Manufactured in the United States of America
Published by Cleveland State University Poetry Center
Department of English
2121 Euclid Avenue
Cleveland, OH 44115-2214

ISBN: 1-880834-70-7
Library of Congress Catalog
Card Number: 2006920109

Ohio Arts Council
A STATE AGENCY THAT SUPPORTS
PUBLIC PROGRAMS
IN THE ARTS
40 Years

ORDERING THE STORM:

How to Put Together a Book of Poems

Contents

Introduction

Several years ago when the local literary center here in Cleveland was opening, I was asked if I wanted to offer a class or workshop. I immediately suggested a panel discussion format and this subject: how to put together a book of poems. This was my literary obsession at the moment, probably as the result of combing my own manuscript's hair in a number of different ways (upswept, disorderly down, in a french braid?). It was one in a succession of problems I'd worried at: how to make a poem longer, how to decide whether something was poetry or prose, where to break the line.

For that initial panel, I came up with a number of questions, by no means exhaustive, of the concerns a poet might have:

1. What should the first poem do? Establish voice, authority, a certain level of seriousness? What are the different ways to invite the reader in?
2. What about the last poem?
3. How long is too long (how many pages of poetry is too many)?
4. In what ways can poems interlock?
5. Are we as committed to resolution as fiction is? Does the ordering have to do with a kind of narrative? Or are there other ordering principles—emotional change, change of approach, change of intensity (mounting?), change of style? Should we offer the best first like the Marriage Feast at Cana or save it for last like dessert? Must there be a direction and change during the course of the book?
6. If a poem is radically different in style, should it be taken out?
7. Which is the more useful question—How do the poems fit together? or What is the whole trying to do?
8. Should the poet think about the reader more when putting together a book than when writing the poem? The reader's commitment will be longer. Does he need

more direction? Should we imagine her picking it off the shelf? Buying after a reading? Has he seen isolated poems in anthologies or journals?

9. How do people read? How do we want them to read?
10. What about the title? If we use the title of a poem, how important should the poem be?

When we have a problem, we look for advice—what do others do? Not so we can replicate their strategies, but so we can listen, consider, begin to make wordless decisions deep in the cerebral mass. It is the conversation that is useful, rather than the single instruction. This quality of conversation, the many voices, is the most valuable thing about this book.

Last spring I asked a wide variety of poets if they'd be interested in contributing to this anthology, if they would send their reflections on the process of assembling a book, their own experiences. In the essays which follow, the reader learns not only how a poet thinks when putting together a collection but also what happens when being a poet intersects with time and livelihood—the poet as teacher, the poet as editor, the poet in change.

Is there one valid way to order your clutch of poems to make them into the best possible manuscript? I don't know. Recently, I was consulting my sister about a particular section of the book I'm working on. I sent her 10 or 12 poems, attaching them to my query as they appeared alphabetically in my list of files. Ignoring the email portion that ordered them, she expressed initial surprise at their jostle, but then came up with a rationale for their alphabet-ness. And maybe being able to perceive a rationale is the key. If the reader can't imagine why this rich bristling portentous poem is placed *here* like a thistle in a smooth green lawn, we're doing something wrong.

Some poems are so thick and knotty that they're satisfying in their stand alone. Some benefit from the support of fellows—clue to clue—or the wash of intimation and emotion seeping from page to page to become more than themselves. Sometimes an outer schema can be pressed into service. One of my most successful orderings was precipitated by an article I'd read in *The*

New Yorker about the musicals of Richard Rodgers. I thought about the poems as if writing a score—overture, song of the ingénue, characters singing their own revelations, comic relief.

There are many metaphors for the process of ordering—it's like a dance, a cartoon, a punishment. The poets kneel on the floor and immerse themselves in their work. And somehow the gathering of the poems results in a kind of baptism—poet and book arise, renewed.

Susan Grimm
January, 2006

Best Foot Forward: Arranging a Poetry Manuscript

——— ***Bonnie Jacobson***

Arranging your poems can feel like herding birds. Or Penelope weaving and ripping. Or analysis. You-the-book will never get it together. Even if you've done it before, this one's a totally different animal. Which is a good thing.

And so you kick back and consult your shelves. There, successful manuscripts are always eager to reveal their secrets. *Emotional cohesion*, some of them murmur. *A singular voice and vocabulary*, others announce. *One metaphor extended so far it finds everybody*, another proclaims. Take heart, these books seem to be saying, romp with excellence and excellence will rub off.

I. Oliver, Klappert, Ashbery, Stafford, Donoghue and Olds

Search the contents pages of Mary Oliver's *Twelve Moons* and, sure enough, scattered throughout this collection of 51 poems are twelve different moon poems. First (although it's the fourth poem in the book) comes "Pink Moon—The Pond." Later, "Strawberry Moon," "Buck Moon—From the Field Guide to Insects," et cetera. Midway, there's "Harvest Moon—The Mockingbird Sings in the Night," until, with the arrival of "Worm Moon," a year has gone by. Such scattering is simultaneously reliable and wild. Nor is it a secret how Oliver learned to do it. In "Flower Moon—How She Travels," the poet tells us flat out who taught her to scatter moons: an unnamed She is seen to "lift from her wagon the Flower Moon" and toss it "high above the trees," then give "another to the shining river." You might say Nature Herself arranged this cycle of poems.

Peter Klappert's *The Idiot Princess of the Last Dynasty* is a much heftier book than Oliver's—205 pages of dramatic monologue from expatriate and occasional abortionist Doc' Dan Mahoney. The flamboyant Mahoney is holding forth among assorted café habitués in Left-Bank Paris from 1939 to 1940. His book is appropriately hefty because Mahoney has a great deal to say about that dark time, and adores saying it. But *The Idiot Princess* is not self-indulgent; showman that he is, Mahoney leaves us wanting more.

John Ashbery's *Self-Portrait in a Convex Mirror* takes its title from the collection's last and longest poem. Because the 34 poems that precede it also contain Ashbery's themes of mirror, art, artifice, experience and time, they point to what's coming—his more fully realized "Self-Portrait in a Convex Mirror." This 16-page reflection, first published in *Poetry*, might have stood alone as a chapbook, but is more wisely the crown jewel of a full-length collection. After all, that collection won a Pulitzer, a National Book Award, and a National Book Critics Circle Award.

Unlike Ashbery's and Oliver's seamless collections, William Stafford's *A Glass Face in the Rain* is divided into sections, five of them. Each of these section pages is filled to the brim with its Part Number (spelled out) and below that THE TITLE OF ITS PART (in large capital letters) and below that an introductory *title and poem* (in italics to set it apart from the poems it introduces). And, preceding Part One, a dedicatory *title and poem* (in italics). Stafford's perhaps overly generous collection—he claimed he wrote a poem a day—like Ashbery's *Portrait*, takes its title from one of its poems, but oh so slyly: "A Glass Face in the Rain" is a twelve-liner buried in the middle of this 98-poem collection. Or rather, hidden like a leaf in a tree, a face in a crowd.

Similarly, John Donoghue's *Precipice* is also the title of one of its poems. However, all 48 poems are irregular sonnets (the only poem longer than a sonnet turns out to be a double sonnet). Like Stafford's collection, Donoghue's book is divided into five sections plus a prologue poem. But there are critical differences: fewer poems in each part; the section pages a stark white except for the lone word "Prologue" or stiff roman numeral; and the physical book, while slimmer than Stafford's, is taller and wider. This breathing space invites the reader to slow down, ponder each step, notice why the next poem proceeds from the previous one. Donoghue's edgy emotional path—that's the trip this book is taking.

Sharon Olds' *The Father* contains 52 poems that can stand alone but together are a daughter's single, relentless ordeal of watching her father sicken and die. And there's more anguish after that, three years of it: cremated and interred, the father's body refuses to surrender its terrible power. *Of course* the persona's messy struggle toward ultimate release is unrelieved by any parsing of it into sections, or adding other sections with other themes, as in the poet's earlier books. *Of course* when Olds reminds us of the biological fact that a father's body lives on in a daughter's, we understand why the final poem is not quite final.

And so on.

And so on because those who write must also read. As our editors, our professors, our fellow poets, our muses and gurus keep telling us: Grasshopper, what you've leapt at and sat down to is one big, ongoing conversation.

So what have you got to say, and when is it time to say it?

II. Your turn

Okay, like Oliver and Whitman, you've found your natural voice, oracular or otherwise. Or maybe you *haven't* found your voice, and that's okay too. (Praised early on for their formal verse, Berryman and James Wright doubted *they* had, and they were correct.) But like Stafford and Frost and Rita Dove, at least you've claimed your territory, even contributed a few pithy remarks, enough poems to fill a book, although you're not really sure—in this case how many is enough? Or, like Klappert, you've been listening ten years to a narrator and characters who won't leave you alone. (In my own case of author-possession, I lived a mere three years with the narrator and characters of my second collection, *In Joanna's House*.) Or maybe, like Donoghue and Shakespeare, a poetic form has seduced you. Or, like Olds and Robert Lowell and others, you're probing emotions in work evidently more than just cathartic because (while you feel you are no Olds or Lowell) some magazines you respect have seen fit to publish bits and pieces of your distress.

Or maybe the whole manuscript came first, and now—if they can stand alone—you're sending out its poems, four at a time. Perhaps in a fever of hope but with no order that really sings, you scoop up your manuscript (even the leftovers) and take it all to a friend whose editorial judgment, like Pound's, is without peer and mercy. Most professional poets I know have one or more of these friends.

That's how my collection *In Joanna's House* got arranged. Or rather, re-arranged. The friend every poet needs was my former professor, the poet/editor/theorist Robert Wallace. For most of his inspired life, Bob quietly performed this feat for a surprising number of prize-winning, internationally-known poets. O lucky *Joanna.*

III. Critical details

This is the material I handed Bob—poems already workshopped, already tested in the national marketplace, even arranged—but in need of his unclouded eye—

Like Klappert's Mahoney, Joanna is a fictional character (though not drawn from rumor and literary precedent, as is Mahoney). She is a dutiful child and then a pleasant wife who shops at Saks and winters in Florida; nevertheless, she has an idiosyncratic interior life, including an occasional tiff with Freud, John Calvin, and others. These events, public and private, are reported by an omniscient observer. And, as Donoghue would do in *Precipice*, all 46 *Joanna* poems use an identical form (26 lines of loosely 10 syllables each). In the last poem (as I had originally arranged the manuscript) Joanna dies, her trappings and her concerns systematically destroyed by a mysterious "We," who declare: "It never worked, *anyone's* identity." And then the deadpan "We" obliterate even themselves. *Joanna* a wisp of time from birth to death, I thought. Ephemera.

But Bob switched the final death poem to a prologue.

What, start with a *downer*? I protested. Didn't you teach us the first poem of a book has to *invite the reader in*? Why plant the Reaper at the door?

Think about it, Bob said. If in the prologue you present *the terrible finality* of Joanna, then doesn't every one of her poems argue *against* that finality? Isn't Joanna's life—and by extension *anyone's* life—a unique and irreplaceable influence? He then divided her life into three sections, took out a repetitious poem, substituted a leftover poem that was okay but needed more work, and moved Joanna's strongest poem to the end of the manuscript. And presto, thanks to my friend's inspired re-arranging, *In Joanna's House* became what I never expected: more than the sum of its parts.

More than the sum of its parts. I think that's what arranging a book of poems comes down to: creating a mega-poem that in some way comments on all the others, or at least takes the poet and the reader a distance from where both began. As Mary Oliver cautions in *Blue Pastures*, "Don't close the poem as you opened it, unless your name is Blake and you have written a poem about a tyger." Especially true of the mega-poem.

Bob found the mega-poem for *Joanna* in less than an hour, if you leave out my fretting. How did he do it? How does anyone do it?

IV. The living room floor

John Donoghue told me he never set out to write a book of sonnets. One day he simply discovered that one of his long skinny poems worked better in that form. And then a short fat one did too. And then he re-fashioned another, and another, because in the turn of the sonnet, "that's where the torque was," he said, "the emotional charge."

Emotion is Donoghue's territory, especially fear. So when John spread his sonnets on his living room floor and knelt as if in prayer (as Bob Wallace had knelt on *his* carpet) it was only natural (something told John) to arrange those poems in "an emotional trajectory": from fear and anger to, in the last section, the softer emotions. Creating that arc—getting to those softer emotions—that's the mega-poem of *Precipice*.

But what about *The Father*, that tale of a parent's cancer and the three years after his death? Didn't Olds have an easier organizational task? Wasn't chronology her obvious structure, or did she, too, kneel a while on her living room floor?

"I don't write books. I just write poems. And then I put together books," Olds told Dwight Garner in a *Salon* interview. Apparently putting together *The Father* was not an easy, straightforward task. At first Olds didn't know if a book with a single subject was a good idea, or if she wanted to tell a story at all; she'd never done either before.

And she wondered if she had enough poems she liked on this particular subject because—unlike many poets—Olds does not write filler poems. But there were enough poems and the tale did want to be told. However, *The Father* is not strictly chronological: some of its poems slip back and forth in time, inserting memories of childhood, revisiting what other poems have already told us, always releasing, reconsidering. Time-as-actor—emotional time—is the mega-poem.

The Idiot Princess of the Last Dynasty is also concerned with time: specifically, Paris from September 1939 to June 1940. In his prose introduction, "A Note on Dan Mahoney," Klappert mentions that his narrator is an American Irishman who came to Paris during World War I and somehow managed to stay throughout World War II (interned or otherwise, Klappert muses). And time doesn't stop there. In addition to World War I, flappers, jazz, Cubism, psychoanalysis, *Ulysses*, Gauguin's cane, and current Nazi propaganda, Mahoney (as razzledazzling as Pound) alludes to the Bible, the Dreyfus Affair, church history, Rilke, Versailles, German children's books, Byzantium, and so much more. Truly a collage of time.

"As the collection grew, the subject of the poems extended well beyond expatriate Paris . . . to the darker moil of Europe . . . and history itself," Klappert recalls. To avoid tedious explanation, Mahoney's elegant monologues "assume an audience in a café which is familiar with French history and with political events between 1919 and 1940." And Klappert himself assumes *an audience of readers* equally familiar with Mahoney's allusions, for there are no footnotes. But perhaps Klappert's mega-poem is not only "history itself," but also our ignorance of it.

So, after a brief holiday with literary friends, there you are—either arranging your poems with renewed patience and insight, or totally intimidated. If the latter is true, well, you *could* dodge the whole arranging thing—just blindfold yourself and shuffle, or pick from a hat. Poets have done this. Or, if you must have order, alphabetize your poem titles. Poets have done this too. But whatever you-the-book decides to do, it's a comment of some kind.

V. Judging the book by its title

John Donoghue says he did not follow the usual rule when the title of a book is also the title of one of its poems. That is, he did not choose his book title because the poem it came from was canonical, or even the strongest poem in his collection. John simply loved the *sound* of the word "precipice." And also the danger lurking there, where John's angst-driven persona feels he is standing.

The fictional Joanna (though not her omniscient observer) worries she is not the good person others expect her to be, which in Joanna's world should include modesty, beauty, chastity, service, guilt, and happiness. Thus, when Bob Wallace wanted to change my title to *The Joanna Poems*, this canonization felt oddly pretentious, unJoannalike. *In Joanna's House* seemed to me a better description of her situation.

Sharon Olds' title is forthright and focused: *The Father.* However, notice the "The" (as opposed to "*A* Father," or "*My* Father" or just "Father"). This article sends conflicting messages of intimacy and distancing: Is *The Father* an individual? A clinical abstraction, possibly Freudian? An archetype? God? As personal as the poems are, *The Father* is shards of all of these, I suspect, and certainly looming.

Likewise, Ashbery's *Self-Portrait in a Convex Mirror* says what it's about even as it sets up its complex extended metaphor.

Maybe William Stafford, like Donoghue, simply delighted in the pure sound and the provocative image of *A Glass Face in the Rain.* Or maybe Stafford's title poem expresses his shamanic wish: to stay, even when he is gone, among the common people he loved.

A shining example of the resonant book title is Mary Oliver's *Twelve Moons.* The moon (like the father) is simultaneously natural and mystical, archetypal and in your blood. It is a metaphor done to death and—in the right hands—always reborn. Oliver's Native-American moons illuminate and reflect her nature-driven poems.

So, as the fella said, whatever you do make the old new, which means yours and yours alone. But, really, short of plagiarism, how could you do otherwise?

Postscript: About advice

A poet once told me his professor in graduate school advised him that when arranging a manuscript of poetry one should always begin by selecting the first, the last, and the middle poems.

The poet said this was no help at all.

It's Simple, Really: Just Sit Down at the Desk . . .

——— *Jeff Gundy*

I. Preliminary Remarks

I have friends whose books of poems seemed to (almost) assemble themselves. One in particular wrote her way through her second book of poems more or less from start to finish, and when she was done the book followed a consistent narrative arc with a clear set of themes and concerns. I don't mean to say that all this came easily; she certainly agonized and struggled plenty along the way. But she had a sense of the overall shape and pattern of the book long before all the poems were written, and actually wrote some of the poems to fill in a gap here or there.

My books have never taken shape this way, though I would be happy if I could make it so. Such a straightforward procedure has always seemed out of reach for me, distractable and restless as I am. It doesn't seem right, given that I've written several extensive sequences and often found myself writing mainly in fairly consistent forms, e.g. prose poems and two- or three-line stanzas, for extended periods. But even when such devices have helped me to generate a lot of poems with something in common (even if nothing more substantial than the look of their stanzas or similar titles) the poems still seem to resist being assembled neatly or smoothly into a manuscript that is either unified, coherent, or precise. Though I have enjoyed or endured plenty of preoccupations and obsessions, even in the midst of these the poems seem to veer off in all directions.

The difficulty of getting books of poems published at all creates another set of weird pressures, especially on a first manuscript. How *do* you catch the eye of a bored, underpaid, and probably inexperienced preliminary judge who's slogging through a heavy pile of manuscripts, much less make yours levitate magically all the way to #1 among several hundred competitors? It's hard not to imagine that there is some mystical arrangement (or some flaky gimmick) that will make the innate magnificence of your work shine out so clearly that not even the dullest reader can miss it. I have many times yielded to the temptation to tinker and fiddle in pursuit of such an arrangement, though often with the uneasy feeling that I was just as likely to be making things worse as better.

Over the many years I spent trying to get a first book published, my "first book" evolved into something almost entirely different than when I began sending it out. I think it did get better, but it's hard to say, really, and if it did it was less because of all those agonizing decisions and revisions I made over the years, I suspect, and more because I was gradually, unevenly, learning to write better poems. Even more gradually, I got some of them published, and finally a publisher was willing to take a chance on my work.

I have found it a little easier—though far from routine—to get books published since my first collection, *Inquiries*, appeared in 1992 from Bottom Dog Press. But if the process of developing a manuscript has gotten easier, that just means I have sometimes managed to do it in three or four years instead of ten or fifteen.

II. My Usual Procedure As an Allegedly Mature Poet

1. Write poems for two or three or five years, sometimes with some sense of a common theme or thread holding them together, sometimes not. These days I often write when I'm out of town, on my way to or from a reading or at a workshop, sometimes when I try out an assignment along with my students.

2. Put all the poems in a big pile. OK, a middle-sized pile. I usually do this too soon, before I have quite enough of the right kind of poems to make a book that's good enough or coherent enough. But I'm impatient, and it's almost like having a new toy to play with.

3. Spend numerous hours, scattered over weeks or months or years, sifting through the poems, making piles, arranging and rearranging. Discover that there appears to be both too much and too little order in the poems: some seem mere echoes of each other, others have very little to do with the rest.

4. Very gradually begin to puzzle out some kind of plausible order. Should there be sections? Often those are nice, but if they are too different, it's jarring, like having a meal that's part Mexican, part Thai, part Italian, and invites odious comparisons. For my second book, *Flatlands* (Cleveland State University Poetry Center, 1995), I began with several sections but then shuffled them together into one long series, creating a kind of weave rather than let them stand lumpily apart.

(Working with the current batch, my interior shorthand for the groups is the esoteric ones, the nature ones, and the sarcastic ones—but all of those categories are at best blurry fictions. Every time through I rearrange them, pull some out, stick in others. Wait—now I have *five* groups, not three, sorted by where I wrote them, not by tone or type. And yesterday, rooting around in old files, I found two nearly forgotten poems that I published in magazines many years ago but never included in a book. They seemed to have uncanny resonances with some current poems, so I printed them out and am trying to figure out if they really belong.)

5. As this is going on, generally, some poems I'm not so sure about get accepted by magazines. Others that I think are grand come back in the mail again and again. My internal ranking of them fluctuates wildly. But gradually a handful come to seem like anchors for the rest, and I start to sense some kind of arrangement. Being the guy that I am, I mistrust anything too obvious, which means just about anything that my daytime mind can understand or explain. So I rely on intuition, guesswork, obscure senses of possible sublimity. But things slowly coalesce until I find myself committed. It's less like crisis conversion or love at first sight than like gradually discovering you're going to church most Sundays and even putting checks in the offering, without being quite sure why.

6. Other questions persist. Are purity and clarity the goals, or delightful complexity? Consistency or range (of effects, of language, of subjects)? Shouldn't I just give the whole thing up and build a new garage instead? I have a Whitmanian desire to eschew consistency and contain multitudes, but I also know what it is to be impressed, then dismayed, and then bored by massive but haphazard accumulations.

7. I fling myself on the mercy of friends and colleagues, ask for their advice about order, about what to leave in or throw out, etc. As I keep telling my students, I've finally *almost* come to terms with the reality that I will never see everything there is to see about my own work. Often they tell me what I didn't want to hear, or what I need to know, which are usually the same.

8. Titles are a particular problem. Of my four books of poems and four chapbooks, the only one for which the title came easily was the one in Pudding House's *Greatest Hits* series, which was called *Greatest Hits*. A good title ought to be evocative but not too direct, and what serves as a perfectly adequate title for a poem often buckles under the weight of a whole manuscript. I usually start out with something lengthy and ponderous, and have to be persuaded to simplify the title and let my typically outrageous ambitions be less visibly announced by the poems themselves. Here again friends and editors have saved me repeatedly: I've had myself convinced that various manuscripts should actually be sent out into the world under the titles "The Sadness of Water and Women," "The Brain Remembers Things That Did Not Happen," and others too embarrassing to repeat here.

9. Beginnings and endings, as we all know, are crucial. As I pondered this, it entered my head that I have half-consciously thought of the last poem as something like a benediction, a sending of us all back into the world with something resembling a blessing. The religious analogy makes me uneasy—I am *not* in favor of the kind of service that ends with an altar call, nor of drawing sloppy equations between poetry and religion, usually to the disadvantage of both. But it may be hard for someone like me, steeped in the rhythms and language of both the church and poetry, to avoid making some kind of connection.

I wonder whether a whole book of poems might not have affinities with a ceremony, a kind of service which would have many of the qualities of a public event to which people come in hopes of some kind of nourishment for their minds and spirits. The explicit language might be "secular" or "sacred"—I'm in favor of keeping the overt God-talk to a minimum and throwing the clichés out completely, though I've not always kept either principle—but

I like that notion. I also like the idea of ending with some intimation of hope, some glimpse of shelter and safety in this dangerous world. My most recent book *Deerflies* (WordTech Editions, 2004) ended with such a poem:

Small Night Song from Oneonta

It's good that the world has more beauty
than it needs. It's good to walk into
the smooth Catskill night and discover

that the night has no edges, no sympathy,
no grievance against me, that any place I step
will hold me firm, not like a lover,

not like a child. It's good to be a child,
and then for years to be something else,
and then something else. It's a hard world

but the rain is persistent, the deer
are quiet and discreet, and for ages now
the trees have known how to dream their way up.

A man with a pack on his shoulder
saunters down the path below me, knowing
the lights he sees ahead are burning for him.

10. The current batch, I'm convinced right now, is either a) by far the best set of poems I've ever written or b) negligible and doomed to eternal obscurity. Maybe both.

III. Closing Observations

How many of us read books of poems in the order they are written, anyway? Generally I flip a new book open to somewhere near the middle and try a poem almost at random, look back at the table of contents, maybe read the first poem, check out the credits . . . unless I'm writing a review or the author is a personal friend, that may be it. Even if I do spend more time with the book, my reading is often haphazard and eccentric. I suspect I'm not alone in this.

Does this mean that all the energy devoted to exhausting arrangement is wasted? I suppose that in a way nothing is wasted, and though I'm not entirely sanguine on this point, at least one part of me thinks that during the time devoted to sorting out and arranging a manuscript all sorts of other kinds of undercover but necessary work may be happening as well. Not much about the writing of poems takes place in the daylight world where sweet reason and order rule, anyway.

The other way I "work" on a manuscript, of course, is by ignoring it completely—not by choice—for weeks, even months at a stretch. The loudmouths who complain that professors barely work have never been employed by small liberal arts schools like mine. This term I have four courses, two on Monday/Wednesday/Friday and two on Tuesday/Thursday, which means that I can and do feel like I should spend more or less all of my daylight time just getting ready for the next class. Then there are journals and papers to read, poems to scribble on, students to advise, meetings to attend; I'm department chair, too, which means another set of duties. Reading for the next day's classes, along with much else, spills over into evenings and weekends, even during the relatively light weeks.

I don't mean to complain—this is absorbing, engaging, rewarding work, it pays a living wage, my office is air conditioned, and my students and colleagues are mostly smart and friendly. It is just a lot to stay ahead of, if it's to be done right. Add in the effort to keep some kind of literary life going, which includes writing individual poems, reviews, essays like this one. Then, of course, there's the need to pay some occasional attention to my family, garden, vehicles, house, and all the other stuff that goes along with modern middle-class life. With all this going on, when do I drag out the pile and ponder and nudge it around? Next summer, or maybe during Christmas break . . .

For long stretches, then, the only work I do on the manuscript is at a long, nostalgic, conflicted distance, trying vaguely to remember what it's all about and which poems I had first and last while walking to and from classes or driving to a soccer game or mowing the lawn. Maybe this is a good thing, maybe not; it's no great cause for self-pity in the big sweep of things, surely. When I read of those like Jane Kenyon and Donald Hall who gave up steady employment for free-lancing and spent hours of most days for years on end at their desks, I wonder what might have been, but this is the life I have chosen to live. In the meantime, or so I tell myself, I'm learning more things, waiting for those serendipitous accumulations that sometimes prove crucial, for the right contest to be announced, for the heavens to open and the Big Friend to say that it is good. Sooner or later, ready or not, I'll patch something together and send it out into the world, and then we'll see.

Journey Without a Map

——— *Liz Rosenberg*

For me, every book of poems is a journey. I think of it as a journey to which I am inviting the reader, and I feel a certain responsibility to each reader, to act as a guide, much as Virgil acts as guide to Dante in *The Divine Comedy*. It is all right to take the reader down into the bowels of hell, if need be, but important to escort them back out again and up into the blue air.

I think it is worth mentioning that two of the greatest books of poems I know—Whitman's *Leaves of Grass* and Dante's *Divine Comedy*—were thirty years in the making. That kind of conviction and patience is rare these days, almost impossible, except for the insane and the saintly. But we could all take a little more time getting our books ready for the world. Poets these days rush poems into books, and rush books into Selected Poems and Collected Poems. Time is the great anthologizer. Time will select and collect, without our two cents' worth.

Beyond the aspect of creating a journey, I have very little system for putting together a book. It is an intuitive process. A book of poems ought to have a dramatic arc—not as obvious as, let's say, a novel or a play, but still present. Just as Frost insisted that all good poetry must be dramatic, I think all good books of poems must have drama—something at stake, a larger meaning, and the feeling that the book, while perhaps composed of smaller stories, is at the same time telling a larger, overarching story. Each book of poetry is a portrait of its time and place, also of the current understanding of what a poem is or ought to be, and of course comprises a portrait of the inside of the poet's mind. Whatever the dramas are—universal, national, or personal, those dramas are reflected in the shape and pacing of the book.

I like a book to open outward. The more personal and particular poems tend to come at the beginning of my books, and the more public and larger poems toward the end. I think our lives do this, if we are lucky. At the start, we are more self-absorbed, and as time goes on, hopefully we become more and more aware of the people and voices and animals and things all around us. We want to open up, like flowers. And our books ought to do the same.

In terms of practicality, I try to start a book with what I think of as a beautiful poem, and to end with a powerful philosophical poem. I think we do begin with beauty and end with wisdom—again, if we are lucky. So the book's journey reflects the journey of our own lives. And yet "there is no path. You make the path in going" (Antonio Machado). I think of this line very often—perhaps more often than any other single phrase of poetry. There is no path, we make the path in going.

Once or twice I have become so addled while trying to pull together a manuscript of poems that I've spread all my poems around me in a circle. The first step is in finding a poem beautiful enough to make a beginning. Then the next poem seems to flow naturally from the choice of that poem. Together, a group of poems begins to tell a story. I like sections in a book, because I feel this gives me permission to tell many stories. Within sections, poems naturally begin to adhere to one another. One section opens toward the next. Once I begin, I seldom have many doubts, because the process has a velocity and honesty of its own. The poem that belongs no place often has no place in the book. Once in a while I'll try to cram something in, but it's awkward, and seldom works out well. Sooner or later that tooth will have to come out. You sacrifice individual poems for the sake of the book as a whole. You find you have repeated yourself. You begin to notice your own frailties. Your tics. Your tricks. All of this can turn the making of a book into an unpleasant process, painful, like therapy.

Once I have the basic shape of the book, I look for what I can cut. I am always looking to discard the weakest poem in a book, and alas, I never lack for weak poems. Even after the book has returned to me between covers—even many years later, when I pick up an old book and begin to thumb through it, I wince at some of the poems I have included. No doubt some of their superior brothers and sisters have been sacrificed along the way. I am not always the best judge of my own work, but I am the only judge I can entirely trust in the end. I ask the advice of only a very few carefully-chosen friends. In any event, I would never want to show a manuscript to more than one or two people. My best readers at the moment are Jason Shinder and Hal Sirowitz. I am amazed at their generosity in being willing to read my work, and to offer a few words about it. They do not offer more than a suggestion, a hint at a direction. They do not try to "fix" my poems for me. Most poets, even great poets give bad or useless advice.

Like most young writers, I spent years asking others for their opinions, and learning how little is to be gained by it. No one else can teach you how to be yourself. This is what we want to do, as artists—to become *most perfectly ourselves.* There is no good becoming perfectly someone else. And it does no one else any good to become our worst selves. So there we are, as we were stuck all along, in the making of each individual poem, and each line in each poem—on our own. I do not trust poets who rely too much on too many other readers. It seems like a strange act of absolving oneself of the responsibility to make the journey worthwhile.

In the end, an editor may weigh in on one or two poems but in my experience editors fiddle a good deal less with one's poetry than they do with one's prose. I would certainly avoid at all costs a meddlesome editor, like the famous New York editor who cut other people's stories down to minimalist bits and, taking an author to lunch, would cut pieces of meat and vegetables off the author's own plate. One must try to avoid cannibals, in art as in life. A good editor may save one some time and trouble. The best editors confirm our own worst suspicions and highest hopes. One's response to editorial comment ought to be "Aha!" rather than "Really?" in shocked surprise.

These are some of my thoughts on putting together manuscripts of poems, and no doubt I have left out some key elements, or contradicted what other poets may find best. But that is really my only point—one must find the path that works best for one's own art. If it works for someone to toss their poems up in the air and see where they land, well and good. That poet may have gravity on her side. We all want to make books we can feel proud of, decades later. We want to make the books we ourselves would want to read. And the only thing that matters in this is not any particular system, or trick or method, but to trust one's own best and unflappable instinct, one's own commitment to the journey.

Finding, Unifying, and Revising the Body of Our Work

——— *Robert Miltner*

When we start selecting the poems to use as the core of a poetry manuscript, one place we can begin is by considering the body of our work. If we ourselves are not familiar with our style, topics, stances, and voice, how can we assemble a collection of our work that will be unified, compelling, and generate interest from editors or readers?

We write our poems, have some of them published, write new ones, all the while, through our experiments, failures, and successes, practicing our craft. Upon reflection, we see we have developed what constitutes the body of our work, that is, the poems, in our own true voice, which explore, in our centered style, the concepts or obsessions which define our work. In constructing a manuscript, we need to assess this composite body of our writing, reviewing both what we have to say and how we say it, so as to determine which poems will make a viable "book" or collection. But how is this accomplished?

If we only take our previously published poems and try to put them together into a cohesive collection, we may find they represent different editorial tastes that reflect the interests of diverse readers, a ragged jumble of poems with no cohesive center. We must ask ourselves, therefore, what are the impulses—the topic, concepts, and obsessions—around which the poems in the body of my work will gather? These impulses, which offer a locus around which to organize a manuscript, may be common or familiar (aging, loss, memory, transformation, for example). Maggie Anderson, editor for the Wick Chapbook and First Book Awards series at Kent State University, looks for manuscripts which offer "something fresh, some take on a theme, maybe, that I haven't seen before, something unforgettable that hits a nerve and stays in my mind." Such resonance is what we might strive for in developing a new angle on a familiar topic.

At this point we need to consider whether the poems which collect around a common impulse are strong enough for assembling a chapbook length manuscript (twenty poems) or one section of a full-length book (fifteen to twenty poems), or are they rich and varied enough to build and sustain a full-length manuscript (fifty to seventy pages). In any case, these impulses, to borrow an architectural concept, become the foundation of a collection of poems. If we are successful in our selection, and find an effective organizing principle, the result will be a collection of poems that has what Stanley Kunitz calls an interior logic, one which is "a composition, a joining of parts into an architectural whole, not just a throwing together of the poems"(11). In essence, what we need to do at this point is to find a form to shape and hold our content.

Our collection can take shape in several ways. One approach is to follow the impulse of the commonalities that seem to act as magnets to which the poems are drawn. Poet Tess Gallagher describes how she operates manually to order a manuscript around impulses: she will "scatter the pages out on the living-room floor and crawl around on [my] hands and knees among them, reading and sensing what should come next, moving by intuition and story and emotion" (xxii). Whether we use the floor or a table, we too can scatter the poems and find the magnetic conceptual pull which will suggest the common impulses around which we can anchor our collections. A number of structural devices can be used.

Often, a collection is lyric, expressing our ideas, feelings, or intuitions; Li-Young Lee's *Book of My Nights* offers an example of such a lyric collection, and Mary Szybists's *Granted* showcases a lyric collection unified with the recurring motif of mouths. Other books are inherently narrative, telling a story, either in a chronological order, as readers find in Rita Dove's Pulitzer Prize winning *Thomas and Beulah*, or in collage as Lee Peterson does in *Rooms and Fields: Dramatic Monologues from the War in Bosnia.* Moreover, the lyric-narrative, which blends the two, offers "the poet's imagination [as] the hero" (Gallagher 74), as readers find in Frank O'Hara's I-do-this-I-do-that *Lunch Poems*, or in Raymond Carver's midlife sobriety poetry beginning with *Where Water Comes Together with Other Water.*

There are, as well, a number of alternative structures which can be used to organize a collection. Lynn Hejinian's *My Life*, for example, offers vaguely autobiographical prose poems connected by recurring phrases; Nin Andrews' *Book of Orgasms* plays with assorted ways to describe metaphoric and real orgasms by borrowing from diverse text forms ranging from definitions to gardening catalogs; and Stephen Dunn's *Riffs and Reciprocities* collects "paired" prose poems—contraries, corollaries, parallels, spoofs, juxtapositions—in a unique experiment that turns out to be a stunning success. Selecting and using one of these four forms, or others, offers a basis for the architectural whole needed to build a collection. Yet, the structure of the collection needs to be more than a large, one-room building; certainly, a warehouse can hold much, but all that space, those endless rows of goods, can be deadly dull. How, then, can we section the structure into rooms out of which the reader can flow in and out, making the structure more aesthetically pleasing?

To borrow an idea from the field of music, we can shift from major to minor key, offering point and counterpoint. We can utilize sets of contraries that give the selected subject of the collection a range of response, either topically, emotionally, or visually, which will enrich our collection. Though by no means exclusive, some of these sets include contraries such as:

art :: life
prose :: poetry
real :: imagined
process :: product
specific :: universal
surface :: depth
absence :: presence
commonplace :: extraordinary
interior :: exterior
speech :: rhetoric
feminine :: masculine
intended :: accidental
past :: present
line :: space
open :: closed
density :: lightness
pop culture :: tradition

Using a set of contraries such as these creates tension, energy, and range, making a well-structured collection richer, fuller, more vibrant. There are a couple of ways to include these contraries in the structuring of a book. On one hand, we can intertwine the two, like two musical melodies, in and out of the collection; as they intertwine, they take turns moving into the foreground or receding into the background, with one sometimes more present than the other. When we do so, we orchestrate the rhythms of the two contraries, so that one of the two contraries is always evident, if not dominant, in the poem. On another hand, we can orchestrate "waves" of the two contraries so that there are peaks of one and valleys of the other, one rising as the other falls.

Further, sets of contraries offer us help in arranging the opening and closing sequences in our manuscript. Obviously, our opening half dozen poems, and our closing half dozen as well, should offer a balance of the two contraries, introducing and concluding, respectively, their interplay. Given that manuscript readers for presses and contests typically read the opening and closing few poems—and sometimes that alone decides which contest entries make the first cut—we should make sure that our opening four to six poems "set up" the rest of the book by what identifies the dominant impulse that is the major key of the collection, along with the mood of the collection, as well as dominant images that will recur, so as to establish a strong voice. We should also read the last six poems, determining how they close out the book by refraining what has been established in the opening. In this way, the collection will resonate, staying with the reader after the last poem is read. Additionally, this structuring method works with a chapbook, a full-length collection, and for interior sections of a full-length work. Having determined the impulses which are at the core of the body of our work, and having identified a set of contraries which give depth and texture to our collection, the next step in the process involves revising the collection for unity.

One way to revise for unity is by connecting the individual poems through variations on some of the images, colors, metaphors, or language which are common to many of the poems, working them in so that a color—blue, for example, shows up as navy blue, ultramarine, robin's egg blue, cerulean, each casting a common tint across a collection. Images of water, to give another example—rain, rivers, creeks, lakes, dew, mist, sweat—can appear in numerous poems, as parts of similes and metaphors, or in combinations, so that "guilt cast a shadow like a long, blue river" brings both color and recurring image together in a simile which is secondary to the moment's concern, guilt. Using this technique carefully throughout a collection both enriches individual poems and binds the poems in the collection together.

A second way is examining how the end of one poem leads into the beginning of the next poem. Connections between the two can be by extension, variation, contrast, juxtaposition of words, images, colors, by endings leading into or contrasting with beginnings. By doing so, the individual poems fit together, moving effectively from one poem to the next as the resonance of the last line—an image, a sound, a word—echoes into the next poem, either in its title or its opening lines, and we can design this transition either to make the movement seamless or to be intentionally jarring through contrast or disruption of the reader's expectation. After all, the book is a body of work in its own right, and we are in position to create the interior logic, the architecture of our collection.

One of the exciting discoveries that emerges from assembling and revising a collection occurs when we find that the unified body of our work suggests new poems. Of course, some of the poems that form the foundation of our collection will be previously published, while others will be under consideration elsewhere, or in draft stage. Yet, once we sense the body of poems that set the foundation for our collection, and we organize, construct, and unify the manuscript, we often find new poems being written just for the collection, poems which find alternative views on a topic, fresh approaches; this gives great energy—often unifying energy—to the collection as it takes shape. Additionally, we may also find ourselves going back to our notebooks for works-in-progress as images, contraries, or concepts suggest we may have poems in draft stage that can be reworked and revised for inclusion in the new manuscript. In other words, after we have begun to organize and unify the body of work with which we have begun, it is in our best interest to remain open to surprising developments—connecting to other work that at first seemed unrelated, inspiring new work—which can contribute to the quality of the manuscript.

Moreover, we can also revise by unifying the titles of the individual poems. When we read through all of the titles on our table of contents, the titles of the individual works can act like an abstract of the manuscript, offering readers a glimpse of the images, moods, themes, or settings that are central to the book. In a narrative or lyric-narrative collection, for instance, as Michael Bugeja recommends, the poet, like the potential reader, can study the table of contents "as if each poem were a chapter in a novel" (125), each title suggesting another scene, development, or point of view to the narrative story line. Yet, this technique works just as well with lyric or alternative collections. Jorie Graham, as a case in point, uses similarly-titled poems in several of her collections: in *The End of Beauty*, she uses a number of self-portrait poem titles—"Self-Portrait as a Gesture Between Them" and "Self-Portrait as Apollo and Daphne"—and figures from Greek myth—Apollo, Daphne, Orpheus, Eurydice, and Persephone; in *The Errancy*, guardian angels—"The Guardian Angel of the Private Life" and "The Guardian Angel of Not Feeling"—and aubades—"Red Umbrella Aubade" and "Sea-Blue Aubade"; and in *Swarm*, nearly half the titles are either "Underneath" or underneath with a parenthetical qualifier, i.e., "Underneath (Always)" and "Underneath (Calypso)." Re-titling poems, or unifying the titles of poems, whether previously published or not, empowers the titles, both individually and collectively, and brings greater cohesion to our collections. Moreover, the process can assist us in finding the title of our collection, whether we select one of the included poems' titles and use it for the collection, as I did with my collection *Rock the Boat*, or whether we take a phrase, image, or line from one of the poems to be the book title, as I did with my Wick chapbook *Against the Simple* or with my forthcoming collection, *Canyons of Sleep*. Ideally, the title poem or title phrase, wherever we have embedded it in our collection, can spark a referral back to the title of the collection as a whole, and resonate through the rest of the book for our readers.

Organizing our poems into a working manuscript begins with finding the central impulse of the body of our work which will be our foundation. Following that, we develop a structure, with enriching contraries, which contains it; this gives our content its form. Eventually, we revise the manuscript by connecting the poems, perhaps generating new poems along the way, as we move the manuscript toward the unity, cohesion, and order which make a book.

Works Cited

Anderson, Maggie. Personal Interview. Kent, Ohio. 22 April 1997.

Andrews, Nin. *Book of Orgasms*. Cleveland, OH: Cleveland State University Poetry Center, 2000.

Bugeja, Michael. *Poet's Guide: How to Publish and Perform Your Work*. Brownsville, OR: Story Line Press, 1995.

Carver, Raymond. *Where Water Comes Together with Other Water*. New York: Random House, 1985.

Dove, Rita. *Thomas and Beulah*. Pittsburgh, PA: Carnegie-Mellon University Press, 1986.

Dunn, Stephen. *Riffs and Reciprocities*. New York: W.W. Norton, 1998.

Gallagher, Tess. "Again: Some Thoughts on the Narrative Impulse in Contemporary Poetry." *A Concert of Tenses: Essays on Poetry*. Ann Arbor: University of Michigan Press, 1986. 67-82.

——. Introduction. *A New Path to the Waterfall*. By Raymond Carver. New York: Atlantic Monthly Press, 1989. xvii-xxxi.

Graham, Jorie. *The End of Beauty*. New York: Ecco, 1987.

——. *The Errancy*. New York: Ecco, 1997.

——. *Swarm*. New York: Ecco, 2000.

Hejinian, Lynn. *My Life*. Los Angeles, CA: Sun and Moon Press, 1980.

Lee, Li-Young. *Book of My Nights*. Rochester, NY: BOA, 2004.

Miltner, Robert. *Against the Simple*. Kent, OH: Kent State University Press, 1995.

——. *Canyons of Sleep*. Philadelphia, PA: Plan B Press, 2006.

——. *Rock the Boat*. White Marsh, VA: All Nations Press, 2005.

O'Hara, Frank. *Lunch Poems*. San Francisco, CA: City Lights Books, 1960.

Peterson, Lee. *Rooms and Fields: Dramatic Monologues from the War in Bosnia*. Kent, OH: Kent State University Press, 2004.

Kunitz, Stanley. "An Interview with Cynthia Davis." *Contemporary Literature* 15:1 (Winter, 1974): 11.

Szybist, Mary. *Granted*. Farmington, MA: Alice James Books, 2003.

Note

Some of the ideas in this essay were discussed in two earlier essays written for the *AWP Chronicle* and *Ohio Writer*.

Poetic Dynamics & the Meta-Lingo of the Manuscript

——— *Wanda Coleman*

For over thirty years, I have survived in the insular small-press world, which, until quite recently, also meant living without the frills, actual or imagined, of a real-live editor correcting one's mistakes, deleting repetitious ideas, condensing one's bloated sentences, or untwisting convoluted syntax. There was seldom a critical note sounded, once a manuscript was finished. As an African-American, published by Black Sparrow Press for over thirty years, I was outside the teensy Black literary mainstream, I was effectively alone in the southwestern United States. To the good, this made me an instant authority on "thangs Black." But there was no Maxwell Perkins in my future. I could "do" whatever I wanted. To the bad, I was undereducated and tended to dismiss even sound advice if vaguely perceived as racist, and did not always know what I wanted, at first. Worse, I was not clear on what my options were when arranging poems or stories into a dynamic order that would complement, enhance or further illuminate them.

Developing poetically required that I get a grasp on my initial sense of an ordered universe, which then seemed multi-leveled at the source: from within (I needed things highly organized in play and work environments); from fairly strict, vigilant and punitive parents; and, from an intense love of reading, calculated to escape the emotional and intellectual damage of the school system in which I was trapped.

Too, there was an overlay and interplay of other creative systems or arts: I was learning ballet (how to rock-and-roll, and how to walk like a young lady instead of a heathen), how to draw and "compose" (develop an eye for the camera's lens), while also learning to read music. What I would later do with all of this "organizational" information confounded me, as I groped to make creative choices. Once I decided on writing, and once I began to focus on developing my poetic style, I began to realize that these other arts were still at work within me, if only up to that point where my study had ceased. Often, I find, upon the writing of a poem, that instead of line breaks, I'm using rests and going up octaves. Instead of juxtaposition, I'm using contour and gesture. Instead of a turn, I'm doing pirouettes. But the major influence on my sense of how those poems, once finished, should be arranged in manuscript form comes from my greatest source of happiness, those pleasurable hours spent reading. Of the many books that gave me pause to consider them in parts (Melville's *Moby Dick*, Horace McCoy's *They Shoot Horses Don't They?*, Baldwin's *Another Country*), my favorites were found in fiction and science fiction (sci-fi), the short story anthologies.

Unlike the usual "boring" arrangement of poets either by year of birth, style or theme of poem, short fiction was more often arranged by concept or idea, particularly the sci-fi, which might elevate an author who would otherwise go poorly noticed. Once I had enjoyed such an anthology, I developed the secondary delight of savoring it, that is, going back over it, cover-to-cover, to figure out what the editors did to put it together. I began to notice that in certain stories language bristled vividly, while others were either flat, or "wafted" with lyricism; that, in the best of these anthologies, the only constant was often that of *quality*, regardless of the author, figurative speech or plot devices. And on top of that, the order in which the stories were organized created a greater, overall dynamic which helped keep the reader interested. That dynamic could be traditionally linear through crises and denouement, jazzily progressive, subtly seductive, or static, like an electrocardiogram. Whatever the dynamic, its ultimate effect is the creation of a meta-language (opinion, philosophy, or world view) that either directly or subliminally informs (and occasionally transforms) the texts assembled.

The work of the editors, I discovered on my own, was not simply to edit a manuscript for craft or technical errors, but included making larger decisions concerning readability or in manipulating the desire to read. Too, the overlay of another editorial sensibility can change the entire manner in which a poem or story is perceived or received. Where a piece is placed in such a compendium sometimes makes a tacit statement about the writer's status, suggests the editor's opinion about any given writer's importance, and reveals the editor's strengths and weaknesses. The editorial process is always organically a subjective one. There is no such thing as the objective, in this cultural instance. Some editors have the uncanny power (or power of crude aesthetic taste) to reduce *everything* they like to pap, in the same way the amateur photographer "shoots" the same basic girl over and over again, no matter how different the bikini, the pose, or skin. The ideal is to have an editor who elevates everything assembled to artistic levels (like, purportedly, Baldwin, Tennessee Williams, and Thomas Wolfe).

Whenever publisher John Martin returned his edited version of a poetry manuscript to me, I was always excited by his ideas about me, or my "image," according to my own poems as he understood them (or his staff, which included an occasional freelance editor). Martin tended to prefer certain aspects (voices) of my personality over others and arranged my poems accordingly. My usual response was "almost got it right." This new first draft allowed me enough distance to revise some of the poems; catch favorite words and delete them, insert better poems on the same theme, take out poems that ceased to work well when new text was added, and to add new text to poems when, in juxtaposition, new text was needed. Remember: my concept of the book was shaped by those wonderful constructs of bound leather, inks, and fine papers that are rarely found even in today's circulating libraries. The digital world threatens impermanence and paperlessness. Yet, in my fantasy book world, those kinds of materials still exist, and when I imagine someone picking up and handling one of my twentieth century books, I imagine their thrill will echo the thrill I felt, in my youth, whenever I hefted a hardbound book of quality and opened its pages.

While I have never concerned myself about manuscript placement in the process of writing poems, where I place each poem, and in which section, become paramount when I sit down to prepare my manuscript for submission to a publisher. I loathe "the grabber" method of storytelling, script, or manuscript preparation perpetuated by the ascension of television and movies. It sells, certainly, but the grabber palls particularly when a poet insists on putting all one's best poems in the front and lumping weaker poems in the back of the ms. without consideration as to the kind of dynamic created, as with small manuscripts submitted for fellowships and grants. What happens, then, if the reader decides to sample poems from the back first? Or to start in the middle? What if someone wants the option to read a creative work in any manner possible? Suppose someone reads the last poem first? (As I used to read the last page first in real crime novels, my least favorite genre.) It would be wise, then, to end one's manuscript on a poem that is an effective summation, yet would engage a reader to know more of the poet.

Once I have selected the title and/or theme, as with the original mss. for *Imagoes* (1983), *Hand Dance* (1993), and *Ostinato Vamps* (University of Pittsburgh Press, 2003), I make my decision as to how many parts and/or sections (usually two and/or four, unless I can achieve that rare moment when the poetry draws the prose to hang together as if each piece is a thread in a weave, as with *Heavy Daughter Blues: Poems & Stories 1968-1988*). These parts or sections have personal meaning and work in tandem with each idea or theme. In *Hand Dance*, I managed to execute an idea originally intended for *Imagoes*, but which was lost in the back-and-forth of the editing process. I wanted one poem to appear at the outset of the book to represent the entire contents in tone, to act as an umbrella, or cast a guiding light over the text (as in the successful opening sequence of *Bathwater Wine*). Additionally, a feedback system evolves from this way of working, as I discover what's really on my mind in the process of framing it for the reader imagined.

My final consideration for manuscript integrity is how the manuscript closes or ends. This highlights another problem with the grabber, because if a book is of any reasonable length, that is, fifty pages or more of poetry, then the reasonable reader is apt to feel cheated or disappointed by the end of the book. Another trick poets use is to intersperse the good poems sparingly and strategically amongst the mediocre and the bad, assuming one can differentiate. I like to make a more sophisticated assumption about my own work, viewing poems in terms of level of excitement, highs and lows, and thinking of their arrangement as a distribution of energy. The order in which I prefer to place my poems often resembles a wave. The poem-action rises and falls, ebbs and flows.

Wanda Coleman

What kind of response do I want the reader to have when they've finished my book, given all possible demographics? Ideally, I hope my reader will be revitalized by the end of the process, gratified, or profoundly moved. I want my reader to perhaps feel the need to linger and savor, or to simply sit with me for a thoughtful length of silence. I want to have touched them, across space and time. I want them to taste my youth and enjoy my sassiness. I want them to be excited by my concerns and ideas. I want them to bemoan my losses and my trials. I want them to sample all life as it has defined me. I want them to have moved through my flesh.

The Shapes a Bright Container Can Contain

——— ***Philip Brady***

A book. The idea of a book of poems. The gloss, the slender spine. A collaboration among poet, artist, designer, editor, reader. Echoing hinted plots, untried paths; yet delicate, brief: the pleasure of an afternoon. It can seem almost an icon from a yet uncanonized hand, bringing news that stays. My first was John Montague's *The Rough Field*, which I came upon in Cork a few years after its 1972 release from Dolmen. How it felt to hold that eighty-four page volume of Times-Roman stanzas with their ominous gaps and delphic montage interspersed with quotes from bedfellows as strange as Che Guevera and the great O'Neill. The solo journey; the cultural undertaking. The noble frontispiece, designed by Liam Miller, adapted from an Elizabethan woodcut of cottages put to the torch, subtitled, "Ulster 1961-1971." The stylized horror framed by calligraphy, "old moulds are broken in the north / in the dark streets firing starts. . . ." The humble grandeur of the opening lines, "Lost in our separate work / We meet at dusk in a narrow lane."

No book but one from that time so resonates, even now, with the pangs of Ulster congealed in a red ink-splash of ancient blood seeping all the way to "streets of Berlin / Paris, Chicago / seismic waves / zigzagging through / a faulty world." My second edition paperback, unearthed in a quayside bookshop, is rusted with rings of Guinness.

Then there was Kinnell's *The Book of Nightmares,* a sequence of ten poems in the voice of a man, "concert of one / divided among himself," chanting into the dark. So many more: Sharon Olds' *Satan Says,* a first book that seemed to emerge from two lifetimes; and Pinsky's *An Explanation of America,* with its Horatian Epistles and porno film critiques, elucidating a father's world to his young daughter, reminding me now of another daughter, conjured in Snodgrass's peerless *Heart's Needle.*

These were not opuses like *The Cantos*, *The Maximus Poems*, *A*, or *Paterson*; they lacked the heft of tomes thick enough to stop bullets. The great modernists didn't crave mere books; they patterned their masterpieces on sacred texts, hermetic, encoded; "poems including history." Neither did the Romantics yearn for the kind of books I'm talking about here. Their longer poems were mythic or pastoral, meditative or Byronic. And of course before that there were the spicy essays of Pope and Dryden, manic with reason, and the epic's doleful drumbeat, marshalling poems, which, as Johnson said of *Paradise Lost,* no one could wish longer.

I won't even get into anthologies. There's something unwholesome about cradling kilos of history on your lap, shifting postures, your thigh going numb, your wrist arthritic. It's overwhelming, all those "great" poems crowding forward like wraiths demanding blood. And the journals tint me envious or enraged.

A Collected? Too definitive. And more than likely it'll offer, instead of apotheosis, the wayward wreckage of a life-plan.

Selecteds? Too much like Greatest Hits. In a time when poems conceive their own form—whether New Wave or Deep Image or New-Expansive or Language or Post-Cereal-Structuralist-Krispies—an anthology or periodical or even a Collected or Selected can swim before your eyes like a petrie dish.

What I want this warm Ohio September Sunday afternoon is a book. A chance to spend some time—but not too much—with a single presence. Such a work, printed while the composition is still warm, reflects one blossoming consciousness, wayward and purposeful, playful, but fully intended. Like a good performance, where each utterance is contained in a thin silence, a book allows a poem to breathe—and surely, amid today's jangle of slogans, Muzak and blather, a poem needs a bright, sturdy container. Not a textbook (who can even read Nortons crabbed with numerals?). Not a website with amebic pop-ups. Not a bus or a radio show. Call me a Luddite, but I want a book.

But how to make one? Can't be too hard. After all, every season sprouts new bushels. Win a contest. Ply a friend. Learn Pagemaker. Spam the market. Buy a stapler. Then stuff verses till they squint. Since most lyric poems aren't composed with a finished book in mind, it may come to that. But when it does, you may find you don't have a book; all you've got is a clot. So you rearrange, fiddle; spread them out over the kitchen floor. You shuffle, dog-ear, append. You phone your pals. If this is your first "kitchen cabinet," your job's even harder, since the poems buttering the tile are the ones that taught you how to write. You love them all, though they get along no better than princely siblings. More elbowing; a purge or two. A few floaters clog the drain. And still no book.

Some say, fashion a book on the same principles which animate its poems; each poem introducing, developing, or recapitulating a theme whose thread runs through the entire work. Fair enough. This certainly makes sense in books which play with or against a traditional form. Scanning a new "crown of sonnets," we glimpse the glitter of crowns from Heaney to Sidney, refracting new surfaces into multi-dimensional shapes. Suspense torques the tension: What new twist? What ploy? Cole unscrews rhyme and meter; Carruth ratchets them up; Hacker turns the gender table; Berryman abra-cadabras table, house, and air. My newest fave is H.L. Hix's sequence, "The God of Windowscreens and Honeysuckle," which raises the crown-tines to a new high—fifty-six. Four seasonal sonnets lend their lines as building blocks to a sonnet for each week. Winter's second line provides the second line for Winter's first week, etc. Such delight in pushing the inside of the envelope.

But what about those poems whose form isn't signposted by shadows? The formative principles of some poems seem so deeply embedded in an original moment that to stretch them over a book would be like racking taffy. How to organize such poems so that each retains its sheath of silence, while cohering into a greater whole? The temptation of course is to segregate according to theme or setting. All poems on the subject of Spring step over here, please. All New Jersey poems over there. Yet, theme alone isn't enough to make a book. Without the compelling tension of a sequence like "The God of Windowscreens and Honeysuckle," how will all these Jersey Springer poems avoid degenerating into a mob?

How to make a book instead of a collection? If your poems are elusive, amorphous, translucent, you might try setting them in a structure that is sturdy, trustworthy, casting its own network of shadows. Inhabit this place. Work its depths. Play on its high wires.

Just as the Romantics housed poems in myth, the Neo-Classicists in essay, and the Elizabethans in epic, our books of poems breathe in the atmosphere of the dominant literary form of the day. And for us, friends, on this side of the millennium, that bright shiny container is the novel.

Think about it. Novels saturate us. They're in movies, on TV, in supermarkets; they claim prime acreage in bookstores; there's a paperback face-down on your bathroom floor, another on your night table. When someone says, "I'm reading a great book," what do you think of? Fact is, whether we like it or not, we're pickled in novels. If you've taught freshmen, you know that their first task is to read a poem as a poem, not a story: "Slow down," we tell them; "Hear the music." Immersed in novels, it's difficult to attend to the nuance, dissonance, misdirection, and systematic derangement that characterize poems. Everything is glossed through fiction's prism.

Not that books of poems should mimic novels, or be held hostage to their conventions of plot, dialogue, setting, and character development. The goal (unless you're Vikram Seth!) isn't to write a novel in poems, but to suggest the feel and breadth of a novel, and in doing so allow each poem to be read in its own eternal time and infinite space.

How can books of poems have the breadth and feel of a novel without billowing into narrative?

First, impetus. Novels hurtle into an imagined universe, impelled by generative lines which seem encoded with the DNA of the entire work: "Call me Ishmael. . . ."; "Stately, plump, Buck Mulligan. . . ."; "Many years later, as he faced the firing squad, Colonel Aureliano was to remember that distant afternoon when his father took him to discover ice. . . ." Borne by self-created logic, their primary sentences feel primal, inevitable, discovered rather than invented. And in this regard, the opening stanzas of books of poems can reveal even more than novels' first lines, since rhythm, line length, texture, and style are highlighted. It can set the theme, as in the unmetered, straightforward opening to Carolyn Forche's *The Country Between Us*: "We have come far south." It can set the emotional tone, as in the last lines of Milton Kessler's first poem in *The Grand Concourse*: "My new job's / to wave them in. / Hello freighter, / hello tanker / Welcome, welcome / to New York." It can introduce voice and conflict, as in Jim Daniels' *Punching Out*: *"This is your first day?* Bush asks. / *I been here 22 fuckin' years."* It can play the first minor-key notes of a symphony, as in Brigit Pegeen Kelly's eponymous "Song": "Listen, there was a goat's head hanging by ropes from a tree." Or it can lay the blueprint for an architecture, as in "Heroic Simile," from Robert Hass's famous *Praise*: "When the swordsman fell in Kurosawa's *Seven Samurai* / in the gray rain, / in Cinemascope and the Tokugawa dynasty. . . ." Books of poems, even more than novels, depend on orchestrated powers which reveal themselves in the first stroke. First lines in first poems are more than first lines of a poem: they are first lines of a book.

Then there's scale. Henry James called novels "baggy monsters," but in fact their girth produces a complex relationship with time. Whether or not a novel is cinched tight, the very experience of reading imposes structure: time in the novel contrasts with the temporal act of scanning pages. Novels distort Aristotelian unities, dwelling for hours in a fictive moment or sweeping through a century in minutes. The overall effect is to present an imaginatively coherent world, suspending or at least counterpointing the reader's quotidian world. When the book drops open on the belly and the hatbrim droops, somehow the novel's world continues to turn.

The best books of poems share this quality. While they don't map a fictive cosmos, they do thread gracefully, relentlessly, through a temporal schemata that may be wildly distorted, but never abandoned. While poems seldom span hours or centuries with the novelistic fabric of "uninterrupted dream," their use of textured sound, linguistic density, inventive typography, and alogical progression intensify readers' focus on the poems as artifice or organism, while at the same time heightening awareness of themselves as beings moving through time: eyes gleaning the page, voices testing syllables. Poems leave us paradoxically *here* and *elsewhere*. Reading too many at a sitting leaves me dazed. When this experience of natural artifice is feathered with a patina of theme, or texture, or thrum of a single voice, it can impart the impression of having read much more than is actually there: the way Ohio rain just feels wetter. Reading a good book of poems is like traveling unknown terrain at night, glimpsing in each lightning bolt a swatch of vastness.

Another way to project scale is through refraction. Earlier I mentioned that besides *The Rough Field,* at least one other great book of poems came out of "The Troubles" in Northern Ireland. I was thinking of Seamus Heaney's *Field Work,* which appeared in 1979. While many of the poems in *Field Work* address the conflict directly, it is the last poem, a translation from the thirty-third and thirty-fourth cantos of *The Inferno*, which expands into novelistic breadth. In "Ugolino," Heaney recounts the fratricidal strife that leaves Florence's traitorous Count "gnawing at [Archbishop Roger's] neck and head / the sweet fruit of the brain." It's a compelling scene of betrayal, imprisonment and starvation leading to hell's frozen cornice, and yet, for all of Dante's bitterness, the poem's placement on the last pages of a book by an Ulsterman writing in the midst of his own hell infuses new meaning into both *The Inferno* and *Field Work*. When Heaney translates, "Pisa, your name is like a hiss / slithering in our country's grassy language," I hear an insinuation of *Paisley.* When he explodes, "may a huge dike / of islands bar the Arno's mouth. / Let Capria and Gorgona dam and deluge / you and your populations," he gives voice not only to Dante, but to his own heart and people. His refracted curse is more powerful than any that could be leveled eye-to-eye; more importantly, it opens and bridges, in two hundred lines, a chasm of five hundred years. How long would a novel take to stretch its legs that far?

The last step is to make a beautiful object. Perhaps because novels are produced by big cost-conscious publishing houses, or perhaps because they feel steam-sealed in words, resistant to other means of apprehension (don't we distrust the adaptation's celluloid bloat?), works of fiction seldom feature memorable covers. But when I think of books of poems that I love, I often think of the cover: the cloud-wreathed Tower of Babel in William Greenway's *Ascending Order;* the don't-try-this-at-home exploding shoes of Nin Andrews' *The Book of Orgasms;* the livid cave-painting of

Robert Lunday's *Mad Flights.* While page counts don't reach triple figures, books of poems can seem large, containing multitudes, in part because cover art opens another dimension, "mirror on mirror mirrored. . . ." Unlike novels, the varied modes of poems permeate the barrier between the reader and "the uninterrupted dream," making it possible to integrate visual art into the kaleidoscope of sensation a book of poems engenders.

Cover art can do more than represent or comment on a book's contents; it can enter into a dialogue, as in William Heyen's *Confessions of Doc Williams*, where George Bellow's pastoral seascape references one poem but also fingers the grain of trim lines running throughout the work. By embracing vision—as well as silence, music, and speech—slender books of poems can feel rampant as any novel.

Running Etruscan Press, an independent publisher of poetry, fiction, creative non-fiction, and criticism, I've had the pleasure of being involved in the making of books of poems, seeing them from manuscript through PDFs to the cartons trucked in from Thomson-Shore. I love tearing through the peanuts, taking in that new-car smell. And holding that first copy, linted with bits of styrofoam, opening the skin-smooth paper to see these familiar poems set in their elegant new typography—it's always a shock, even after the proofs and galleys. It wasn't until I touched the gunmetal jacket of Heyen's *Shoah Train,* featuring the eerie smokestacks and bestial engines of Samuel Bak's *Trains,* that I felt the full impact of those magnificent poems.

H.L. Hix's *Shadows of Houses,* Etruscan's newest book, came to life in the penumbra of Sarah McKenzie's aerial-photo-miming oil painting wrapping around the cover in a design conceived—like all our books—by the talented artist, Elizabeth Woll. The painting's strange perspective almost prepares the reader for the sinister permutations of Hix's genius. Bruce Bond's *Cinder* first came to Etruscan under another title. Bruce mulled several possibilities, each casting a slightly different light on the book's nuanced, complex poems. When he came upon *Cinder,* he also found the painting which would adorn its cover, *The Isle of the Dead,* by nineteenth-century artist Arnold Boecklin. Title, image, and poems formed a new book, nascent but unseen until they coalesced.

And speaking of *Cinder,* other great titles come to mind: Charles Simic's *Return to a Room Lit by a Glass of Milk,* Amiri Baraka's *Preface to a Twenty Volume Suicide Note,* Bill Knott's *Autonecrophilia,* Tony Hoagland's *What Narcissicm Means to Me.* So much better than "Something and Other Poems." Come to think of it, why must a book be titled after one of its poems at all? Of the books I've mentioned here, *The Country Between Us, The Rough Field, Punching Out, Cinder,* and *Shadows of Houses* all found their titles in the interstices between poems, as did two of my books, *Weal* and *Forged Correspondences.* In my case, I didn't find the titles alone. Somebody found them with me.

Assembling my own "kitchen cabinet," I was lucky enough to have a novelist and a painter on call. Sounds like a set-up for a joke, but it led to some of the most serious work I've ever participated in. While I sorted poems by zipcode: Ireland, Africa, Queens, California, the Psyche; my novelist was knocking around in the crawlspace, soldering pipes and valves. Thumbing through that book from ten years ago, I still enjoy opening to a random page to see how Bob Mooney found the thread between poems that had been composed in different times and moods. Another thing he taught, yelling up from that psychic underground: cut till you bleed.

Some midnights I still find myself apologizing to ghosts turned away from the table of contents. But listening to Bob's voice, I learned not only about putting a book together, but about making the next one. Now, however intense my attention on the moment, I attend to the floorboard's vibrations. I can't put the feeling into words. But I don't have to, because there was someone else in that kitchen, working (almost as hard as I'm working this damn metaphor) on the roof. His name is Bob Carioscia, and images of his paintings have appeared on three of my books. Always, at one time or another during the making, I take a trip to his studio in Little Italy, where I find a magical store of dream-visions to array old poems and to generate new ones. One hangs above my desk. It portrays a house outlined with real twigs and embedded in a fiery sky above a fish-infested sea. Inside the twig house is a painted one, and inside that, a man holding a picture of a man.

Is it a book? A secret? A soul? In the flaming sky appear the electrified words, NOT KNOWING, RELYING ON INTUITION.

Good words to make books by.

Order & Mojo: Informal Notes on Getting Dressed

——— ***Beckian Fritz Goldberg***

The poet putting her first collection together often believes there is a black magic to ordering her manuscript, some perfect order that will convince an editor or contest judge to publish the work, an order that creates unity, clarifies connections between the poems, minimizes the flaws and maximizes the impact. Nothing, it seems, causes more anxiety and superstition. Many times I've seen a poet whose ms. is rejected or praised but rejected ("Dear Finalist. . .") obsess over structure.

There must be some way she, or he, can shuffle the poems again, rethink the progression, divide into three sections or change to four sections, or move the poems he or she is most secure about to the front, or perhaps bunch all the poems about mother together, then the poems about the Midwest, then the poems about erotic adventures, or maybe sprinkle them throughout the ms., ad infinitum. It's like getting ready for a date and changing one's clothes ten times beforehand trying to get the right look—not too dressy, not too casual, not too much cleavage, not too little, black shirt or the deep blue, one button unbuttoned or two, hair moussed or natural, jacket/sweater/what goes best with these shoes. The insecurities are the same. We are convinced if we make a wardrobe misstep, our date won't find us attractive. If we put our poems in the wrong dress the editor won't be seduced.

It's scary because it's true. It's also true there is no one right dress. Poets putting together a first book are particularly prone to want some sort of formula. Some mystical method. Spread all your poems on the floor. Walk around reading them. Group by tone, group by chronology, group by looking at it as a geography of textures. "Never put peeing elephants on opposing pages" (Norman Dubie). Work from the last line of a poem to the first line of the next. Alternate long poems and short poems. When I was first putting a ms. together I listened to every piece of advice hoping

I'd find something that would work its magic and unify the book.

Most advice was useful in helping me to think of my work as a body, of the relationship between poems. As a first book is commonly a collection of everything-decent-you've-written up to that point, the tendency is to reject "earlier" poems or to perceive earlier work as too different a voice to integrate into the whole. Usually this is just another imaginary windmill. Inevitably, because we write from our obsessions even as our work evolves in tone or voice, there are stronger linkages than we initially perceive. It's helpful for that reason, to ask a couple good readers of one's work to look over the organization of the ms. once you've come up with a possible order and ask for suggestions. Offering to help organize a friend's manuscript is also instructive, since we often learn more readily by trying to structure someone else's work. It's informative to look at books one admires and look closely at how those books are structured. Take a look at how repetition is used in Jean Valentine's *The Messenger*, how the following through on a particular set of images works in Linda Bierds' *First Hand*, how the sections work in concert in Larry Levis' *Winter Stars*, how one archetypal image informs Nancy Eimers' *No Moon*. And take a look at Ted Hughes' *Crow* to see how he organizes by voice and tone.

Dividing the manuscript into sections is often the most manageable choice for both reader and writer unless the poems have been written with a conscious governing order or unity, such as a seasonal cycle, or a narrative progression (such as David St. John's *The Face*) that requires no interruption. Otherwise, think of sections like chapters in a good novel. The closing of the chapter may resolve one series of developments but usually it also foreshadows a new set of circumstances or possibilities.

The most important thing is not "imposing" an order, but discovering the relationship between the poems and letting that suggest an ordering. You can't organize a ms. like Louise Gluck's *Ararat* unless your work lends itself to the sort of narrative arc or progression that her lyrics do. But a book such as Michael Burkard's *Fictions from the Self* wouldn't lend itself to the same sort of architecture. This has to do with "finding your mojo." Beyond pragmatic considerations such as opening with a strong poem that pulls the reader in, prepares them for the journey ahead, and dividing the ms. in sections that open and close with poems that speak to one another, or front-loading (putting all your big-gun poems up front) your book for the contest circuit, the best order for a manuscript is one that suits the personality of the work. If you're Cher you can wear a sequined Bob Mackie gown. If you're Willie Nelson you'd better try jeans and a T-shirt. So you wouldn't necessarily put your ms. in a tight dress if you are an expansive poet like Larry Levis or Gerald Stern and you wouldn't wear blue jeans and an old T-shirt if you were, say, Anna Akhmatova.

While working on my first book, I was in a class taught by poet Jack Myers who talked about Yehuda Amichai's collection *Great Tranquility.* Early in the book there is a poem about the death of Amichai's father and then, much later, a poem that begins with the reappearance of his father (a ghostly one it turns out) in a local café. The effect of this placement created a palpable pleasure for the reader—this moment that recalled an earlier moment in the ms. and let the reader feel not only the ongoing presence of loss among continuing experiences, but provided a sort of touchstone for the reader, a reminder. It was a discussion that made an impression on me and I often think of it when faced with organizing a manuscript even now. Had he grouped the two poems together, the impact would not have been as strong as it is with the later poem revisiting (and revising) the poet's loss. The surprise of the father's "return" is more potent for its removal from the original poem about his death.

In recent years there's been much fuss about the order of Plath's *Ariel,* Ted Hughes' version and Plath's original. The fact is that *Ariel* is a powerful book either way, but each version presents a slightly different overall vision. At the time Hughes arranged the ms., it had to have been difficult, if not impossible, for him not to be influenced by the effect of Plath's depression and suicide and that is reflected in the arrangement. Plath's version, ending with the famous "bee poems," reflects more of a life-force and, perhaps, a more aesthetic vision. In most volumes, the arrangement of poems can make a kind of "arc" or journey and there is not only a single possibility in the work, but several.

With the pressures on aspiring poets these days to enter the "poetry lottery"—those rounds of competitions offering publication to the winner—there's a profound anxiety about finding the right order to please or persuade a contest judge. And though I've had occasion to judge some of these contests myself, I believe it's misguided to think you can "psych out" the contest judge by arranging your poems in a particular order. One judge, for instance, may like a thematic grouping of poems—section I, Childhood & family poems; section II, Love poems, etc. I tend not to trust these arrangements in most cases. I like to see some range from the beginning. I like to be persuaded by the poet's voice rather than his or her categories. Those are my tastes. Another judge will have her own. It also doesn't mean that any judge can't be persuaded by a fine book no matter what her or his usual preferences about structure. So it's most crucial that a poet ordering a manuscript is true to the work rather than to any perception of what so-and-so might like. One wants to engage the readers of course, but you can't do that unless you have a sense of what's at stake in your own work and stay true to that.

With a first book it's a particularly daunting challenge. At least with a second or third you have some experience of trial and error to build on, and usually more of a sense of having written toward a body rather than simply gathering together a collection of poems written your first year in grad school alongside poems written five or six years later without a thought of how they related to a whole. I shuffled that first ms. after every contest season wondering what I had to do to "break through." I remember at one point I concluded that I simply wasn't being "obvious" enough, as much work I saw getting published seemed to be almost painfully obvious about its "themes." But what were my themes? Why weren't they obvious enough? Or was there something about the nature of my work that simply didn't lend itself to the prevailing (as I perceived it) aesthetic?

With subsequent books, I had a better idea about the general "territory" of the work, connections between the poems, as I usually just began writing in the dark until I had a handful of poems I was relatively satisfied with, and frequently they did cluster around my current obsession. And obsessions are as good a place to start as any. They may not always be "topics"; sometimes they are smaller elements, less conscious elements. Certain words may reappear or certain images (such as images of water, or animals in an urban setting, or processes such as demolition, or gardening, or textures—as in Mark Doty's work, a work full of glitters, luminosities, glowing colors). Sometimes all you need is to discover a sequence of four to five poems that form a pleasing cluster for you as a reader. Once you've arranged these five in a sequence, it can open up possibilities for the work as a whole. Look for the elements of repetition in the poems, whether it's a phrase, an image, a sound, a setting you return to, a central question that keeps arising, and consider what kind of architecture gives these elements the most impact.

Taking the time to select a title for the book that conveys some metaphoric property or governing tone is an integral part of structuring a volume of poems. Flaccid titles such as *House of Memory*, *Waking in the Light*, or one word titles such as one's favorite noun or verb don't give you much to go on. They convey no real attitude and evoke no palpable image. It's difficult to construct a book around a vague or generic title even if it's loaded with meaning for the author. Most of the time, for me, the title is key for the book's identity and a touchstone for determining a structure.

The concern with the ordering of a poetry manuscript seems to be a contemporary neurosis. It's doubtful Keats stayed up all night debating where to put "Ode to a Grecian Urn" and where to put "Lamia" in his volume of poems. Dickinson simply put the poems in a trunk. Others died early and left the whole pile for literary executors to sort out. But poor Whitman couldn't get past the first book and kept reorganizing. And as we have an ambition for each poem we write, we should have an ambition for the book as a whole. Dress accordingly. Beyond that we should remember, as Donald Hall so wisely stated, that the desire to write poems that endure is a goal undertaken with only two certainties, "that in all likelihood we will fail, and that, if we succeed we will never know it."

An Invitation to "Invisible Guests": The Poetry Collection as Existential Project

——— *Karen Kovacik*

Finding a publisher for my first full-length book of poems, *Beyond the Velvet Curtain* (Kent State, 1999), took nine long years. At one time or another, the manuscript had four different titles, and it changed shape many times. Now, when I review earlier versions of the book, I feel reactions from astonishment to horror. The sensation is not unlike seeing photos of myself from the Seventies where I'm wearing brown and rust plaid bellbottoms or olive paisley culottes. But the comparison to decades-old snapshots is not only about aesthetics. Those first versions of my manuscript reveal what I had not yet learned, ways I had not yet suffered. In short, the story of the book from inception to publication is deeply existential.

Like many first books of poetry, mine began as a Master's thesis, called "Old and New Testaments." I had little sense of how to compile a collection, except for hearing William Stafford say that when he had enough poems, he spread them out all over the floor, then gathered them into thematic groupings. So that's what I did. The earliest version of my manuscript fell into three sections: American Alchemists, a loose set of poems featuring U.S. locales and characters; Unhappy Families, alluding to Tolstoy, which dramatized incidents from my own immigrant clan and from Polish families I had met in Warsaw; and Old World Alchemists, a suite of poems inspired by European film, literature, and art. Out of 33 poems in that first version of my manuscript, only 12 made the final cut in the eventual book.

What accounted for this dramatic revision? The short answer is that I needed to undergo intellectual, spiritual, and emotional growth—that is, I had to experience certain kinds of suffering in order to write many more poems and to learn better how to put together a collection. Seven things in particular prodded me to revise my manuscript over and over during its long years of limbo:

1. My original title was taken by another poet.
2. I became a screener for book contests.
3. Around the twentieth anniversary of the Watergate break-in, I began and completed a suite of poems about Richard Nixon.
4. Working on a dissertation about twentieth-century American women poets from working-class backgrounds helped me see my life through the prisms of race and class in addition to that of gender.
5. After a twelve-year hiatus, I returned to the Catholic church.
6. I began teaching creative writing full-time.
7. Maggie Anderson's editorial suggestions inspired a final recasting of the manuscript.

All of these things—catalysts, if you will—forced me to see my material through multiple lenses, which helped me better envision how readers, including hostile ones, might receive my work. Each of these catalysts helped me transform my unpublishable thesis into a published book. And by the end of the process, *Beyond the Velvet Curtain* represented less some sort of career accomplishment than a hard-won emblem of vocation.

The first item on my list—losing my title to another poet—initially seemed like terrible luck, though in the end, it forced me to come up with a more fitting title for my collection. The other poet, Lynn Powell, belonged to my Cleveland writing group, and when we discovered our manuscripts were both called "Old and New Testaments," we made a pact that whoever got her book accepted first could have the title. That turned out to be Lynn—a good thing, because in retrospect, the title fit her manuscript about her Southern Baptist family better than it did my fledgling book, which meandered between Eastern Europe and Chicago.

Titles, always important, are especially useful in honing first books of poetry, which are typically assembled over a longer period than are subsequent collections and thus are more difficult to organize. Because titles broadcast tone and sensibility, they must be resonant, but they should also provide a focus and suggest overall structure for the book. To assist the book title in performing these many functions, I'm fond of titling each section of the manuscript and including epigraphs at the beginning of my books.

Unfortunately, the two titles I came up with after "Old and New Testaments"—"Einstein's Train" and, then, "Dreaming Détente"—were too abstract. The first, referring to Einstein's many train metaphors in his General Theory of Relativity, I hoped, would suggest the relativity of perception in my poems about family, history, and art. But finally that entire concept came to seem too vague, even banal. The other title "Dreaming Détente" felt syntactically awkward—should it instead be "Dreaming of Détente"?—and too remote. After the Cold War officially ended in 1991, the word "détente" dropped out of common usage, and younger readers, some of whom would be screening my manuscript, might indeed be unfamiliar with the word. Nonetheless, because I couldn't think of anything better, I kept "Dreaming Détente" as my title for several years.

In September 1997, a year before my manuscript was accepted by Kent State, I deliberately set out to create a better title. Because of the evolving manuscript's theatricality, its emphasis on moving in and out of personas, I decided I wanted to include the showy word "velvet" in the title. My journal from that period includes long lists of runnersup such as "The Velvet Portmanteau," "Communiqués in Velvet," "The Velvet Envelope," "Raise High the Velvet Curtain," and "The Velvet Frigate." When I finally arrived at "Beyond the Velvet Curtain," I could see that it resonated with "Iron Curtain," important in a book that contained many references to Eastern Europe, and with a theater's curtain, but that it also suggested a more metaphysical or metaphorical boundary. This "velvet curtain" might in fact represent the irrevocable border between giving birth and not giving birth, between life and death. The new title's arc of resonance made it immediately seem right to me.

Truth is, I might not have realized "Dreaming Détente" and "Einstein's Train" were clunky titles had I not been a screener for book contests. For the poet struggling to order a manuscript, there is no better activity than combing through a box of 30-60 would-be books, from which only one or two will be passed on to the final judge. This harsh, Darwinian exercise taught me to read with a merciless eye, starting with the title. Did it make me want to read on? Did it contain unremarkable language or near cliché? Did it seem too broad ("A Potpourri of Poems")? I never eliminated a manuscript solely because of its title, but I admit that certain titles prejudiced me against the books attached to them.

Even a "small" box of manuscripts contains some 1800 pages of text. Although in an ideal world, a screener would read every word, the truth is that few do. My method was to read the first few poems of a manuscript. If those seemed engrossing, formally interesting, and thematically rich, I would keep reading. If not, I would skip to the last few poems. If those, too, seemed unremarkable or dull, I would either stop reading or take one final sample from the middle of the book. I came to realize that the first and last few poems of a collection are crucial slots for conveying a book's worth to a potential screener.

Being a screener clued me in to why my manuscript had been rejected more than a hundred times and taught me to analyze my book more carefully. Helpful comments from my friends Marilyn Annucci, Susan Grimm, and Jesse Lee Kercheval aided me in the process of weeding out weak poems, substituting stronger ones, and making the overall order more logical. I learned to start with material that would suggest the major themes of the book, but would also be idiosyncratic enough to stand out when compared to 30-60 other first poems in a box of manuscripts.

One such poem, which became the opening of *Beyond the Velvet Curtain,* was "Nixon on the Pleasures of Undressing a Woman," which I wrote as part of a series about the disgraced ex-president some twenty years after the Watergate break-in. Nixon exerted considerable influence on American politics—occasionally for good, more often for ill—for nearly half a century, and I wanted to foreground how his beliefs in détente and *Realpolitik,* how his unabashed "end-justifies-the-means" manipulations, intersected with earlier versions of such ideas during, say, the French Revolution or the American Civil War, and also with incidents from my own life. In my reinvention of Nixon, he was a figure of indeterminate gender, uncertain of his masculinity, and ill at ease sexually. Poised between Europe and America, loathing his own body, my Nixon represented the liminality suggested by the phrase "Beyond the Velvet Curtain."

However, the Nixon suite also posed some problems for the book. After writing the series, which also included poems from the perspectives of Nixon's wife, Nikita Krushchev, and the Nixons' dog Checkers, I began to fear that I was escaping into personas too often. Having read Alicia Ostriker's anthology *No More Masks,* I became aware that in some versions of "Dreaming Détente," half of the poems in my collection were written in a voice clearly not my own. At the time, this tendency seemed problematic, so I vowed to write more explicitly out of my own life, "in my voice," for a period. Drafting my dissertation about women poets from working-class backgrounds helped me to find the formal strategies and rhetorics, and even more, the intellectual background to do so.

Since the 1970s, I had become used to viewing my life through the lens of gender. I recognized misogyny when I saw it, and I thought of myself as a feminist. But class, as Paul Fussell tells us, "is America's dirty little secret." When I had started college in the late 1970s, almost all the poets we read were white men who had elite educations, as if poetry belonged exclusively to them. I had come from an Eastern European, working-class family, and most of my male relatives had worked in the machine shops, steel mills, and refineries of northwestern Indiana. People like that were nowhere to be found in Eliot or Stevens or even in the work of Elizabeth Bishop, my favorite American poet.

Initially, my doctoral studies alienated me both from my fellow students, some of whose grandparents held PhDs, and from my family, where only one person of my parents' generation and no one of their parents' generation had been to college. I can remember parties involving extended family where I kept the conversation going by plying cousins and uncles with questions about their lives, but no one asked me a single question in return. I had somehow lost the thread of how to talk to my relatives, or they to me.

But working on the dissertation gave me concepts like the "rural to urban migration" or "the costs of upward mobility," which I could use to rethink the story of my white ethnic family. I saw anew my grandmother Mary Kovacik enthralled by that professional immigrant Lawrence Welk. I recalled dozens of Polish jokes that I had heard as a child with the new understanding of how they had made Polishness itself a joke, an identity subject to ridicule. I looked on my mother with new eyes as she, ever the perfectionist, rolled out the sticky dough for our Christmas Eve feast of pierogi. And working on the group of ten poems inspired by my dissertation research, I felt myself learning my past differently, claiming it, seeing my family as both conforming to archetypes of race and class, but also departing from them in idiosyncratic ways. All of the languages of childhood, Polish and Slovak and Latin, came swirling back to change me and my poetry. My dissertation research—and the ensuing poems—opened up the canon for me in a personal way by allowing my family to be written into literature.

But I probably would not have finished the dissertation or begun the suite of family poems had I not returned to the Catholic Church in 1993, after a twelve-year hiatus. My relationship to that institution is too complicated to address here in full. Suffice to say that as a feminist and a person committed to gay and lesbian rights, I am still deeply troubled by the institutional Church. But I also know that the Church is more than the institution. It's the multicultural congregations, the questing for social justice, and the mystery of the sacraments. During my long sabbatical from the Church, the language of the Mass, which I had learned by heart as a child, was always available to me. Memorizing the Mass and certain prayers had been my first experience of poetry—that is, it taught me about the values of pattern and repetition, and it imbued words with near magical powers.

Over time, without the regular rituals of Catholicism, I found that I had become overly dependent on psychological explanations for things, and I longed for communal manifestations of awe. And so I went back to the Church, and the effect on *Beyond the Velvet Curtain* was most evident in the poems I wrote about my failed marriage: the title poem, "Illinois," "Shortwave," and "Tureen." Without the undergirding of that shared Catholic ritual and the conversations with my spiritual director, Sister Wanda Wetli, I would probably not have had the courage to revisit this part of my past.

Teaching full-time also helped me bring my book closer to completion. Suddenly I found myself having to prepare twelve different courses and to forge connections between reading and writing. Some assignments were quite simple: having students write odes to ordinary objects in the manner of Pablo Neruda or giving them a little bag of ten "magic" words, rich in specific nouns and active verbs, that they would then weave into poems. But others required more intense scrutiny and more complicated instructions. If I required my students to imitate Elizabeth Bishop, for example, I would first do so myself, so that I could break her style down into comprehensible components. Bishop's mastery of the three-beat line, her fondness for using color, and her fusion of the homely and the beautiful (such as the "pink swim-bladder" likened to a peony in "The Fish") I understood more deeply only when making her work accessible to my students. Or, when teaching Seamus Heaney's *North,* I refamiliarized myself with the history of English and learned about pivotal events in Irish history because I wanted my American students to experience this important book both as historical creatures in a country that cares little for its history and as poets who would ideally use words with sensitivity to how and when they entered the language.

Often, I do writing assignments with my students, and a couple of these experiments found their way into *Beyond the Velvet Curtain.* "Revising Sylvia"—about Plath—was inspired by a visit to Indiana University's Lilly Library, where I took a group of students to look at the poet's early manuscripts. We came up with an assignment to scavenge lines that Plath discarded from her poems. I chose the suggestive phrase "gaping its inaudible white cadence" for a poem in which I imagine Plath leaving Hughes for a woman in 1959, based on some textual clues in her journal. In my poem, Plath survives!

Beyond the Velvet Curtain was selected by Henry Taylor for Kent State's Stan and Tom Wick Competition in July 1998. By this time, the manuscript was in four sections— "Statecraft," "Mastery," "Feast and Famine," and "Exile"—each rather rigidly defined. "Statecraft," with its allusion to Machiavelli, contained only the Nixon poems, while "Mastery" was exclusively about artists, and so forth. Maggie Anderson, general editor of the Wick Poetry Series, asked me to consider shuffling the order a little. "Statecraft," in the published version, incorporated "Miss Victory," a poem about a feminine icon of war, atop an Indianapolis monument; "Illinois," a poem about my former husband's cultural background; "Citoyen," an erotic lyric, which made use of French Revolution motifs; and "Breslau," a poem about the layeredness of a city, now Polish, formerly German. These changes personalized the section somewhat, drawing connections between my version of Richard Nixon with other icons of domination and revolution. I like to think that this thematic broadening from section to section made the book more dynamically resonant.

Writing this essay has not been easy. And now that I'm nearing the conclusion, I find myself thinking of the maxims that T.S. Eliot, in "Tradition and the Individual Talent," presented to poets: "The progress of an artist is a continual self-sacrifice, a continual extinction of personality." And later: "Poetry is not a turning loose of emotion, but an escape from emotion; it is not the expression of personality, but an escape from personality. But, of course, only those who have personality and emotions know what it means to want to escape from these things." At different times in my writing life, I've hated those words, have understood them to mean that poetry must be devoid of passion—something that even a cursory reading of Eliot would reveal to be untrue. But now I am able to hear the phrase "extinction of personality" in a more mystical guise. Just as Buddhists believe that we must give up attachments to all aspects of the self that prevent us from a compassionate identification with others, so, too, we as poets must renounce certain egocentric mannerisms, certain habitual ways of making poems, or risk stagnation. Sometimes, as I discovered when writing the poems about my family, "giving up the self" means "writing the self more complexly and vividly into being." At other times, it means understanding how we can extend the self by projecting ourselves imaginatively into others' lives through the use of analogy or persona. That is why as an epigraph to *Beyond the Velvet Curtain*, I chose an excerpt from Czes^{3}aw Mi^{3}osz's "Ars Poetica?":

> The purpose of poetry is to remind us
> how difficult it is to remain just one person,
> for our house is open, there are no keys in the doors,
> and invisible guests come in and out at will.

I find Mi³osz's notion of the difficulty of remaining "just one person" deeply comforting. Writing *Beyond the Velvet Curtain* taught me how to leave the house of poetry open. And the "invisible guests," when they came, helped me revise more than mere poems.

A Reply to Storms: How Some Collections Were Ordered (or Disordered)

——— *Carolyne Wright*

Each collection of mine seems to have found its way toward an ordering principle that emerges organically from its subject matter and formal qualities. I touch on the exploratory nature of this organization with terms like "finding itself" and the tentative-sounding "seems" because I want to point to the importance of cooperating with the material and its essence, of not trying to impose organization but of allowing it to reveal itself. At the same time, though, I observe that my more recent collections are conceived of as whole books, rather than as assembled collections of individual poems. These more recent books are largely narrative and story-impelled; and in one manuscript currently in progress (a "memoir in poetry"), the sequence of poems is chronologically ordered, following events in the lives on which the poems are based. Such has been my evolution as a poet and arranger of poems into collections. Another influence was the notion of the "lyric sequence," subject of a text by Sally Gall and the late M. L. Rosenthal, with whom I studied in the early 1980s. According to Gall and Rosenthal, poems are linked in a book-length ordering by their inherent lyric, as well as dramatic and narrative, properties, to create what they called a "liberated lyrical structure."

More recently, I have been edified by Natasha Sajé's notion of "gesture (Latin, to carry) as a trope for a book's organization: How does the book carry itself, and how does it move the reader?" According to Sajé, gestures are movements and designs in the arrangement of poems within a manuscript that signal authorial intent and focus. These gestures include "opening strategies"—thematic, imagistic, linguistic, rhythmic—that can "seize the reader's attention" and welcome her into the world of the poet's imagination. Sajé is particularly interested in the autobiographical gesture, which "negotiates between self and subject" to place the poet's identity within a social context. Indeed, she posits poetry as "alternative autobiography"—not a "correlation of identity and biography," but a series of gestures in which the relationship of the poet to her poetry remains "deliberately oblique." In my case, I have contemplated these gestures in retrospect, not while putting a book together, but in order to write about the process of putting together the books discussed here.

My first book, *Stealing the Children*, is a series of lyric-narrative, mainly free-verse poems selected from the miscellany of my Syracuse University Master's thesis manuscript. For this collection, I found myself grouping poems not according to their dates of composition ("*Poems 1972-1976*," for example), but according to the personae and voices that inhabited them, and the thematic concerns that impelled their creation. The lyrical voice of this early poetry explored what Donald Dike in his Introduction to *Stealing the Children* called "the human nexus," amidst Northwest and Rocky Mountain settings that "map and re-map the inner life of ongoing relations with others and with oneself."

The book is divided into two (numbered but not titled) sections, the first section "mapping" the inner transformations of the life of the spirit, including the dynamics of relationships with friends and lovers, as echoed in the contours of the landscape. The second section undertakes a journey across the physical landscape of the speaker's native West, including the movement outwards from the family of childhood into adult life and family relationships. But which poems fell into which section was not determined by a logically imposed ordering or an external examination of subject matter. It simply "felt right" to order them as they are—to begin the book, for example, with an ironic *ars poetica* of setting forth in dedication to the life of the imagination (which turns the speaker from a "secretary to the thoughts of others" to a "tenured scholar of all galaxies"). It "felt right" also to follow "The Cosmic Scholar" with a poem involving a hike along the Pacific coast as a figure for the inner journey, then a poem taking the metaphor of a long-distance drive to map a spiritual trajectory.

Sometimes an image or phrase in one poem presented itself, or a variation on itself, in another poem; such a likeness of image or similarity of tone would cause me to place two poems side by side in the collection to heighten the resonance of the sequence. In this way, the poems arranged themselves organically in a harmonious flux. The book concludes with a "Prayer," humorously echoing the Lord's Prayer, in which the speaker and her companion ask to be allowed to make an extraordinary inner life together amidst ordinary external circumstances. In turn, the Higher Power encourages them, in the speaker's imagination, to persist despite distractions and discouragement—that is, to keep living, to "breathe on."

The poems in *Stealing the Children* were influenced by my rainy, fir-and hemlock-shaded, mountain- and inlet-ringed Seattle childhood; by the brooding presence of ancestors of the Northwest indigenous people, who had only in the last few generations relinquished their territory to the onslaught of white settlers; by my travels throughout the Western U. S.; by early readings of (and in some cases, study with) poets of the "Northwest School": Madeline DeFrees, Richard Hugo, Carolyn Kizer, Theodore Roethke, and William Stafford. After I moved East to pursue degrees in the Creative Writing Program at Syracuse, this "lyrical Northwest" voice began to modulate to a more "East Coast" tonality. When I recall the occasions of their composition, I realize that nearly one third of the poems in *Stealing the Children* were actually written in the East, but under the still-forceful momentum of the Northwest speaker's voice.

Another matter that can influence a collection's organization is manuscript length. *Stealing the Children* is 41 pages long, which according to some criteria categorizes it as a chapbook, 48 pages being the minimum for a standard book-length edition of poetry. The policy of Ahsahta Press at the time, though, was to publish books of about 40 pages in length—perhaps as a cost-saving measure. Accordingly, after they accepted the manuscript, the Ahsahta editors asked me to reduce the number of poems in it. Working together some months later, the editors and I finalized the Table of Contents by cutting about a dozen poems, mostly those not as close in theme or tone to the book's core concerns and the Western subject matter of the volumes published by Ahsahta Press, hence not as likely to be "missed."

However, neither I, the young poet glad to be publishing her first book, nor Ahsahta's editors in the third year of this publishing venture, realized at the time that less than 48 pages could qualify Ahsahta titles as less than full-length. Prior publication criteria for a scholarship that I held at the Bread Loaf Writers' Conference a year later was for a chapbook, and in my Bread Loaf Scholarship bio paragraph in the conference brochure, *Stealing the Children* was called a chapbook. Nevertheless, the book has a spine, not the chapbook-format folded-over, stapled or sewn binding. It was marketed, reviewed, and acquired by bookstores and libraries as a full-length book.

I never thought to reintroduce poems cut from *Stealing the Children* to make for a new, standard-length edition, because I had already incorporated them into another manuscript, *Premonitions of an Uneasy Guest*. Most of the poems in this manuscript were written between when I first arrived in Syracuse, and when I completed the doctoral dissertation manuscript upon which *Premonitions* was based, thus many of its poems are contemporaneous with those in *Stealing the Children*. I submitted *Premonitions* for a few years to the publishing contests extant then, and it was ultimately a finalist in the AWP Award Series. At the time, AWP circulated its finalist manuscripts to presses with which it had a cooperative publishing arrangement, and one of these accepted *Premonitions of an Uneasy Guest*.

This collection, now out of print, is 67 pages long, but there were major production problems with the press that published it. The first issuing of the book was far below industry-standard production values and thus unacceptable both to me and to the AWP. After receiving the first shipment of author's copies, I recall stopping in the open hallway between the mail room and an administrative office of the small, conservative college where I was teaching, to tear open the package. I was so appalled at the poor quality of the books inside that I burst out with an "Oh, S__t!" so forceful that the poor secretary in the office jumped several inches in her chair, almost knocking the Bible beside her typewriter to the floor. Lengthy phone calls ensued to the press's director and managing editor, as well as to AWP—calls in which I gradually recovered from my initial shock and emotionality, found myself standing up for the professional production standards that publication in the AWP Award Series was supposed to guarantee, and resisting all excuses or attempts to persuade me to accept the crummy printing job.

Reluctantly, to fulfill their legal obligation to AWP, the press's editors agreed to reprint the book to correct the worst flaws. But even in this improved version, the primitive binding made for odd ridges at the folds around the spine, the sans-serif font was more appropriate for advertising fliers than for poetry, and the cover stock was an easily soiled white and not sturdy. Because the budget for the book was basically depleted by the first sub-standard issuing, the second printing was for fewer than 500 copies—which, according to most criteria, made it a limited edition: another publishing anomaly. This book was virtually dead on arrival, or so I felt. I could sell it at readings, and by then I felt that the sooner it sold out the better.

To keep my spirits up after such a disappointment, I called this second book a "transitional" collection, but I did not want to send it out as a writing sample for creative writing teaching job applications—I felt that a poorly produced book would worsen, not improve, my chances of being offered a position. Beyond the production challenges, this book was indeed transitional—it included most of the poems cut from *Stealing the Children* for length and thematic considerations, plus others from my master's thesis and my recently completed doctoral dissertation. To order this miscellany, I had arranged it into five sections according to subject matter, each with a title taken from one of the key poems in that section: "Choosing My Name" (poems about identity and the evolution into an adult sense of self); "The Discipline of Becoming Invisible" (poems about the inner spiritual quest expressed in terms of travel); "Eulene" (ten poems featuring this anti-heroic alter-ago); "Premonitions of an Uneasy Guest," the title section (poems exploring the nuances of romantic relationships); and "Vital Connections" (poems exploring the nuances of friendship within family and within romantic relationships).

Looking at the collection now, I would collapse the first two sections into one, and likewise consolidate the fourth and fifth sections into one, since the subject matter between related sections is not really all that different. So perhaps it was just as well that this book had limited distribution.

As for the "Eulene" section—I would either leave her as she was, the deadest of dead centers for the book (I never refer to Eulene without ironic hyperbole), and by far the most troubling and interesting section in the collection; or I would remove her and give her a venue of her own. This is, in fact, what I have done—confecting a full-length collection (tentatively entitled *Woman, Money, Watch, Gun: the [Not Calm But] Collected Eulene*), which involves the misadventures of this whimsical alter-ego. This collection is organized more or less according to Eulene's spontaneous (or utterly contrived) generation, development (arrested, indeed tried and convicted, development!), and maturation into the nuanced, culturally subversive entity into which she has morphed. Since I am still editing and rearranging this book, though, I will save the rest of this discussion for a later time.

By this point, the publication of both my first and so-called second books qualified, according to some rubrics, as a chapbook and a limited edition, respectively—they represented such atypical and exceptional publishing circumstances that very few publishing contest organizers could determine what their actual designation was. Before sending to competitions for second or third books, on several occasions I had to query managing editors and explain these circumstances in order to learn whether I was qualified to submit. Fortunately, the ostensible third collection, *Seasons of Mangoes and Brainfire*, won the Blue Lynx Prize, an open competition for poets at any stage of their publishing career, so the status of earlier collections didn't matter. With this collection, I hoped that I would be out of the clutches of the printer's devil!

Seasons of Mangoes and Brainfire began as a grouping of poems that dealt with the year I had spent in Chile on a Fulbright Study Grant, and also traveled elsewhere in Latin America, during the courageous but doomed presidency of Salvador Allende. In this year, I came into contact with people whose individual lives were indelibly altered by immense social and political events, the larger forces of history that ultimately swept some of them away. On September 11, 1973, a year after I returned to this country to enter graduate school, Allende was overthrown and killed in a U.S.-supported military coup. Much of the poetry I wrote in the ensuing months was affected by the parallels I was discovering between the Latin American and North American social stratification and the influence of public events and historical forces, particularly in the lives of the disadvantaged. Hence, a number of poems from this period (their early drafts included in the master's thesis or doctoral dissertation manuscripts) explored the dynamics of marginalized lives in the United States: in inner-city grade schools, remote Native American reservations, and small-town, working-poor neighborhoods. Others I wrote later dealt with the lingering effects of the Holocaust and the legacy of wars in Europe and the Middle East. A few of these poems moved from other collections in progress because their subject matter seemed more appropriate to this manuscript's overarching social, cultural, and political concerns.

When I first put it together in about 1993, this collection was entitled *The Lost Addresses*, from a line in the manuscript, a title which seemed appropriate because so many of the poems dealt with the sense of exile and estrangement, the dislocations and losses incurred in a world where larger historical forces divided people from each other. The poems grouped into three sections—the first contained poems set in the U.S. and Europe, the second section poems set in Latin America. The third section was comprised of a single long poem, "Flowers in Winter," set in Europe during the Iran-Iraq War, and chronicling what Maurya Simon (who selected the poem as winner of a major narrative poetry competition) called "an American woman's devastatingly brief, yet permanently affecting, encounter with a Near-Eastern stranger." *The Lost Addresses* concluded with a section of Notes on the Poems, to clarify for the reader unfamiliar with the historical references and backgrounds of some of the individuals portrayed in the poems.

I submitted *The Lost Addresses* to publishers and publishing contests, and received some polite expressions of admiration from editors, and a few finalist designations in the competitions, but no acceptance. Then, at the Vermont College Postgraduate Summer

Writers' Conference in 1998, poet Roger Weingarten looked at the manuscript, expressed enthusiasm for it, and said:

> I'm not going to give any line-editing suggestions, because these poems are finished. But here are my three pieces of advice. First, lose the title and find a more evocative one somewhere in one of the poems. Second, get rid of the subject-matter-driven sections, and the awkward, clumping effect these create, and allow the book's implicit narrative to move back and forth between poems set in Latin America and those set in Europe and the U.S. Third, start the collection with "My Last Night in Bahia," because that poem really allows the reader to enter the world the speaker evokes and through which she moves. Then, follow your instincts however they take you in ordering poems after that, but make sure to alternate between Latin America and other settings.

Energized by Roger's suggestions and encouragement, I took *The Lost Addresses* apart, in a scenario often evoked by poets who recount how they ordered a particular collection: I spread all the pages out on the floor and moved them around, the better to perceive relationships among poems of imagery, diction, and voice. As Roger had advised, I put "My Last Night in Bahia" first, then allowed the relationships between imagery in individual poems, and my sense of the atmosphere evoked by each one, to determine the placement of each successive poem.

I decided on two sections, with all the poems except "Flowers in Winter" in the first section. It was liberating to break out of subject-defined sections, and weave the manuscript together in a lyrically impelled narrative arc, beginning with the Bahia poems, and moving out from Brazil in ever-widening circles across the literal and emotive landscapes invoked in the poems. Sometimes the connection between one poem and the next was as direct as a linking word or image. The last line of "Victor Jara (1932-1973)," for example, is "like a story from someone else's life," and the first line of the succeeding poem, "Survivor's Story," is "A high wind blows across your life." These poems are inversely linked as well, in that the first is a tribute to the renowned folk singer arrested, tortured, and murdered by General Pinochet's thugs after the military coup in Chile; and the second is a tribute to a young man whose family survived the Holocaust and emigrated to the U. S, but who is still haunted by the enormity of the dislocations he had experienced. "Survivor's Story" ends with an image of trains returning from the front; the next poem, "Sierra Walk," found its placement because it begins with the speaker stepping off a train, the "Cuzco-Machu Picchu local."

"Flowers in Winter," originally the third section of *The Lost Addresses*, remained as the second and final section. Because of its length and division into twelve sections, it worked better as an entity unto itself, and the mood of longing and melancholy on which it concludes felt like an appropriate note on which to end the book. With its opening poem ("My Last Night in Bahia") that recollects a final event, and its concluding poem that recounts an inconclusive relationship ("lovers who never meant to go home unfinished"), the book resists closure, and this ongoing openness to possibility gives the book, and the journey it traverses for the reader, a momentum that flows back out to the world from which it came and which it exists to represent. Or at least that's how this collection appears to me now, in retrospect, as I have contemplated the process of putting it together.

Following Roger Weingarten's suggestions for a new title, I read through the poems for an evocative phrase or image that would leap out, and when I came to the phrase, "Our season of mangoes and brainfire" in the poem "Josie Bliss, October 1971," I knew I had it: *Seasons of Mangoes and Brainfire.* After submitting it to about a dozen more publishing competitions with spring 1999 deadlines, in August of 1999 I received the phone call from Lynx House Press editor, Christopher Howell: "You've won the Blue Lynx Prize." Relieved and gratified that the lengthy submission and waiting period was over, I looked back through my file of letters from competitions, and saw that the older version of the manuscript had been a Blue Lynx finalist in the previous year. Reorganizing the poems and giving the collection a new title had indeed made a difference in this competition between finalist and winner.

Organization of the manuscript did not end, however, with prize and publication. The final judge's recommendation was to delete the Notes on the Poems, because they made the text too lengthy, and I acceded to this suggestion. But after the book appeared, many readers and reviewers of the first edition felt that the Notes were needed, to serve the purpose I intended: to clarify the background of persons portrayed in some of the poems, and to explain historical allusions and cultural references embedded in the language, especially of the poems set in Latin America and Europe.

Winner of the Blue Lynx Prize as a manuscript, and after publication, the Oklahoma Book Award in Poetry and American Book Award from the Before Columbus Foundation, the book's first edition sold out, and since it was doing so well, the publishers determined to reprint it. In the interim, Lynx House Press had become an imprint of Eastern Washington University Press, acquiring a higher profile and the advantage of a more extensive distribution network. In fall 2005, *Seasons of Mangoes and Brainfire* was reprinted as an Eastern Washington UP/Lynx House Books title. With the Notes on the Poems and some other missing material restored at my request, a new ISBN number, and a few changes to the book's cover, the new printing is technically a second edition, not merely a straightforward second printing.

The most recently published collection, *A Change of Maps* (Lost Horse Press, 2006; Idaho Prize 2nd), is not at all the newest in terms of composition. From the writing of the first draft of the oldest poem to the completion of final revisions of the newest poems, there is a span of over twenty-five years, and the manuscript has gone through more transformations, title changes, and reorganizations than any other collection of mine to date. The earliest poems are extensions of a sensibility that began in *Premonitions of an Uneasy Guest* and are, I think, completions of what I was trying to accomplish in the *Premonitions* voice. The early lyric personae from the first book reappear, but a few seasons older now, matured and made wiser by disappointments with spiritual quests and a few romantic relationships. Indeed, the voices of these more mature personae, who fuse lyric allusiveness and humor with ironic social awareness and cultural themes, are the principle unifying factors that have determined the inclusion of poems in *A Change of Maps*.

Another characteristic of this collection is a greater prominence of form, signaling my increasing interest in and reliance on formal patterns in poetry—partly as an homage to some of my mentors, particularly William Blake, Elizabeth Bishop, Madeline DeFrees, Emily Dickinson, and James Wright, among many others—and partly as one strategy to enhance the intertextuality, the web of echoes and allusions, both linguistic and formal, to the poetry of those who have inspired me. The most resonant of contemporary poetry is engaged in a dialogue with the tradition—with the voices of poets who have gone before—and to the degree that a contemporary poet reads and is informed by these earlier voices, her own voice develops, enriched and enlivened by what she absorbs and how she responds. Attending a graduate writing program while free verse was still the dominant, indeed default style, I felt a need, similar to that which James Wright noted in his recently published letters, "... to commit myself to the traditional syntax and the traditional meters of English verse; for many of the writers who preceded us were so sloppy, that we had to begin not by revolting against competence and restriction . . . but rather to begin by creating *our own* competence."

Influenced by New Criticism, many American poets of the generation prior to my own wrote in traditional form—the early work of Maxine Kumin, W. S. Merwin, Adrienne Rich, Anne Sexton, W. D. Snodgrass, William Stafford, and of course James Wright himself demonstrates this fact. But when they taught the younger generation—my generation—I wonder how many of them imparted any of their early formal training by assigning exercises in the sonnet, sestina, villanelle, and the like? How many taught classes in craft for poets? Nobody I ever worked with, except Elizabeth Bishop—ironically, she stated at the outset that she didn't like teaching, and didn't know how to teach, but we would at least learn something of practical use in her class! So we wrote in form, one exercise after the other, in that workshop—the only graduate creative writing course in which I ever received such instruction.

Among the formal structures available to poets are nonce forms and variations thereon, particularly abecedarians and rounds. The opening poem of *A Change of Maps*, "Studies with Miss Bishop," is a double abecedarian, a series of 26 slant-rhymed couplets, one couplet for each letter of the alphabet—not a form that Miss Bishop herself ever used, but one intended to enable a narrative disciplined and intensified by the sort of formal containment she would, I hope, have appreciated. In the last few years, I have written a number of rounds, several of which are included in this volume. Like the musical rounds we sang as kids ("Three Blind Mice," "Row Row Row Your Boat"), and the more sophisticated Baroque fugue, the round uses repetition and repetition-with-variation of motifs or compositional elements. These elements are interwoven in a relatively free manner over the course of a few dozen lines, with new elements entering at intervals, and concluding with the same line (the opening motif) or a variation on the same line with which the round began, to create what I believe to be a lyric resonance not as available to straightforward lyric-narrative, or to the more rigidly structured sestina.

Even when not writing in form or modified free verse for *A Change of Maps*, I focused on symmetry and balance, putting poems into regular stanzas, though these were largely unrhymed and not in any fixed meter. Partly in reaction to what I felt were too many shapeless-looking free-verse poems in the transitional volume *Premonitions of an Uneasy Guest*, this later collection that grew out of it features several poems that appear formal: their stanzas divided into tercets, quatrains, cinquains, sestets, septets, octets, and dectets. Most of these poems achieve a sense of intrinsic order with a regular number of stresses per line (but without strictly counting stressed and unstressed syllables to measure feet), and in only a few poems, with slant rhyme. Thus the formal look is mainly just that—a look—and not truly a demonstration of rhymed and metered *terza rima*, ballad quatrain, *rime royal*, or whatever.

Over the years, often after exchanging manuscripts in progress with other poet friends, I rearranged poems in the collection and changed its title in response to these friends' suggestions and according to several different ordering principles. Having saved many of the successive Tables of Contents, I find it interesting to compare them and trace the manuscript's evolution. Originally entitled *The Custody of the Eyes*, the earliest manuscript had 36 poems (in two sections of 18 poems per section); as I wrote new poems in the 1990s and early 2000s that seemed to adhere to the same sensibility, I added them to the manuscript, which grew to 42 poems (21 per section), and then to 46 (23 per section). At one point, entitled *Daughters of Albion* to emphasize an aesthetic debt and connection to William Blake, the manuscript was organized into four sections named after books or poems by Blake ("Innocence and Experience," "The Idol Virtues of the Natural Heart," "Daughter of Memory," and "Daughter of Albion"), with each section's title page featuring a relevant epigraph from a Blake poem. This arrangement was quite satisfying in some ways, but I soon realized that it was too artificial a construct, given that the subject matter and settings, as well as the sources of influence of the majority of the poems, were American, not English. Later, at its most expanded version and by then entitled *Under the Sign of Cancer*, the manuscript contained 51 poems, all in one continuous lyric-narrative arc, with no sections, according to one reader's idea of linking the poems by key-word or key-image, in a structure akin to M. L. Rosenthal's notion of the lyric sequence, according to the associative thematic and imagistic links resonating from each poem to the next.

The focus on symmetry, harmony, and formal properties with which I put together this manuscript highlights an ever-increasing awareness of the reader: particularly of what might be attractive for the first readers and judges for book publication contests. In fact, as the number of contests (and entries to contests) multiplied over the years, I grew acutely conscious—perhaps overly conscious—of these issues. Of course, with the wide range in taste and sensibility of first readers and final judges, it is also true that much was left to chance. Through its many incarnations, the manuscript was a finalist several dozen times (more than once in some competitions), and came tantalizingly close in a few instances—as runner-up in competitions that do not publish both winner and runner-up, but only the winning collection. Then there was the unforgettable "case of the disappearing publisher"—in which the manuscript (at the time entitled *Under the Sign of Cancer*) was invited and then accepted for publication in a new series, and even received a $1000 advance, before the poetry series was terminated by the publisher's new corporate owners.

A few days of despair ensued, before I determined to take advantage of this chance to revise and further strengthen the manuscript. Working from extensive comments and suggestions of one poet friend with whom I exchanged manuscripts; I reordered the poems yet again, emailed a list of half a dozen poem titles (including all those that had already served as the collection's title) to another poet friend, then changed the title to *A Change of Maps* based on that poet friend's preference. I kept sending it out, and soon thereafter, it was accepted by Lost Horse Press as a finalist and runner-up for the first Idaho Prize. After all the experiments and re-orderings, the final Table of Contents is not too different in its scope or lyric-narrative arc from the earliest arrangements, except that more than before, with the opening and concluding poems ("Studies with Miss Bishop" and "The Custody of the Eyes") the collection emphasizes with humor and pathos the author's debt to and distinction from her poet-mentors, particularly women poets. The poet's ultimate aesthetic and social gesture, then, is to inscribe herself with optimism and confidence as a member of a vital and ongoing literary tradition—a tradition she intends to carry forward into the future.

Works Cited

Ali, Agha Shahid. *Ravishing Disunities: Real Ghazals in English.* Middletown, CT: Wesleyan University Press, 2000.

Rosenthal, M.L., and Sally Gall. *The Modern Poetic Sequence: The Genius of Modern Poetry.* New York: Oxford University Press, 1983.

Sajé, Natasha. "Dynamic Design: The Structure of Books of Poems." *The Iowa Review* 32 (5) (Fall 2005): 149-162.

Wright, Anne, and Saundra Rose Maley, ed. *A Wild Perfection: The Selected Letters of James Wright.* New York: Farrar, Straus & Giroux, 2005.

Throwing Poems at an Editor to See If They Stick

——— ***Amy Bracken Sparks***

I wish I could say my book of poems, *serious red*, was something envisioned, carefully planned, plotted and placed. That it was the finish line of a fifteen-year marathon. But plotting—sister of positioning, the nice cousin of scheming—isn't in my vocabulary.

Like every opportunity, every gift that had been proffered, I didn't quite believe this offer by the Cleveland State University Poetry Center to publish a collection. I didn't win a contest; didn't enter one. It was 1995 and I had been out of graduate school for 13 years.

I had early luck: *American Poetry Review* accepted the first poems I sent out, with a request to send more. Other publications followed: *Southern Poetry Review*, *Denver Quarterly*, *Nimrod*, and more local and regional publications. I think I received one rejection letter, from *Prairie Schooner*. Luigi-Bob Drake and his Burning Press (Lakewood, Ohio) published a small edition of my work titled *queen of cups*, with cover art by artist Holly Morrison.

In 1991, at the urging of the late poet Daniel Thompson, I started slamming poems for the Cleveland team. I had been reciting poems by memory for more than a decade; slamming them came easily. I traveled and teamed with wonderful poets like Daniel Gray-Kontar, Ray McNiece, and Michael Salinger, but stopped three years later when I realized what I wanted to write couldn't be performed in a three-minute, competitive "slam" situation. In 1994, I wrote a series of ten poems for a one-time performance called "Esorotica," inspired (or outraged) by the European witch-hunts, about which I researched and prepared for six months, an ascetic repetition of reading, writing, working-out, and meditating in a mostly empty house. "Esorotica" was performed in June 1994 at Cleveland Public Theatre.

Those poems were written to be spoken aloud. Created for an audience that may never hear them again (much less re-read them on the page), they had to have aural punch rather than crafted lines. Highly dependent on sound, emotion and unsubtle imagery, illustrating ideas which listeners could grasp immediately—even viscerally the ten "witch poems" were explosive. They also coincided with an implosion; I stopped writing. For the next nine years, I wrote approximately twelve new poems.

I don't remember the date when Dr. Leonard Trawick of Cleveland State University called to say they wanted to do a book. I'm grateful to Leonard for being exceedingly patient with me.

I gave him everything I had, like opening wide a door to my house, which I never do. The work wasn't a full, well-ordered sequence. The poems in *serious red* are small clusters of series poems: eight somewhat Petrarchan sonnets written about people I know, titled "Fourteen Stitches"; a largely ungrouped set of poems thematically strung together by the confluence of the body, the city, the Cuyahoga River and Lake Erie.

Some poems represent incomplete series: a potential twelve-part series based on the months of the year yielded only "February." February was so depressing, I couldn't go on. Then there is the "disease" series, consisting of three poems and two diseases, "The God of Asthma," "Anorexia Nervosa," and "Lungs."

Several poems were written in a series reinterpreting Greek myths: "Penelope" waiting for Odysseus on the near west side of Cleveland, "The Mourning of Icarus" about an old couple in Tennessee mourning their son, and "Psyche" concerning a starving street cat. There are several persona poems or poems about specific women in history: the artist Ana Mendieta, Frida Kahlo, Joan of Arc, all tragic and heroic. Included in this list is a poem about and dedicated to my mother, Barbara Fenwick Sparks, also tragic and heroic.

While this may sound like chaos, there is a through-line in the book. The female body is the organizing principle in *serious red*. The poem "Morph," the second poem of the book, sets everything up. The description of it sounds brutal: an angel's wings are cut off, multiplied twice, and placed in a female body as a pair of lungs and the double curve of the pelvis. I usually ground my interest in the mythic with something earthbound. "Morph" concerns vestigial wings and the search for spirit as breath.

I "cleaned up" several performance poems to be read on the page. This involved removing some repeating lines or refrains from the poem, shaping it and often adding new lines. The shape of these poems on the page is discernible: they are longer and skinnier than poems that have thoughtful line-endings or enjambments or are structured in couplets or triplets. Since performance poetry relies on the breath, not the concept of a line, line-endings can remain arbitrary, or may just serve as mnemonic devices for the poet's breath-memory. (Although some performance poetry can transfer easily to the page, and all poetry benefits by being heard aloud, I believe performance poetry is a whole different animal, one that must take into account the physical voice and presence of the poet; charisma, voice training, and choreographed gestures can carry a poem that may be lackluster on the page.)

Leonard graciously went through the pile I gave him, cutting and ordering. At his request, I included the very early poems "The Horticulturist," "Counting," and "Feast Day" that were published in *American Poetry Review.*

As I look back on it now, the raw, open-woundedness of certain poems must not have sat well with him. (Some don't sit well with me now, ten years later.) We would meet periodically. I don't think I had much to say. I did offer a vague idea for the cover—an image that conveyed bones and flesh and the female body—and Leonard knew exactly what to use: a collage of plates by Andreas Vesalius of Brussels, *De humani corporis fabrica* (1543), used in the design by Frank P. Cucciarre. The cover image, in my mind, pulled everything together.

I stalled a long time when he asked for a photo. For *American Poetry Review*, I sent in a four-photo set from a photo booth. This time, in desperation, I had a photographer friend, Anastasia Pantsios, take a photo on the stairwell where I worked. I gave my meanest, most pit-bull face. I still avoid looking at that image.

After I threw everything at Leonard, and most of it stuck, we came up short. Not quite enough for a full collection. That's when I showed him the *Esorotica* "witch" poems. He chose the ones that looked most like poems, even the foul-mouthed ones that I can't read at most readings, the ones that include children or family in the audience. The original ten "witch poems" were honed down to six, and they became the center sequence of the book, arranged in the same order in which they were performed. They are tough, uncompromising, and raw. They had never before been published. Leonard, and CSU, took a chance.

Because I had stopped writing, it seemed a small miracle when the book arrived. I know *serious red* is not a big seller for the CSU Poetry Center. (It's not even a small seller.) It doesn't show up on the Local Author shelves anymore. I sell a couple here and there out of my car. It seems more a document of a certain time, a placeholder, a palimpsest.

When I now hold it in my hands, it's amazing. I'm currently writing better poems, studying poetic sequences, and reading highly organized, sequential, all-of-a-piece collections: Louise Glück's *The Wild Iris*, Diane Gilliam Fisher's *Kettle Bottom*, Natasha Trethewey's *Bellocq's Ophelia*, Cornelius Eady's *Brutal Imagination*, and Robert Gibb's *The Burning World*, books that are singular works of art, rather than a group of poems framed by a front and back cover.

I would say that my experience is not the way to go about putting a collection together. But it happened, and I give Leonard, that soft-spoken Southern gentleman, all of the credit.

Keeping Company: Thoughts on Arranging Poems

——— *Maggie Anderson*

> *I been making quilts for a long time. . . . We made them out of old clothes, old socks, and then after other people went to work at piece factories, if you had somebody related to you, they would get you pieces. I don't follow no pattern. . . . I was just doing the best I could. When you sit down you got to get yourself a mind of your own, figure out a way to put them together.*
>
> — Geraldine Westbrook, quilt maker of Gee's Bend, Alabama, interview with William Arnett, 2000

> *The process of writing a poem represents work done on the self of the poet, in order to make form. That this form has to do with the relationships of sounds, rhythms, imaginative beliefs does not isolate the process from any other creation. A total imaginative response is involved. . . .*
>
> — Muriel Rukeyser, *The Life of Poetry*

I know I am on my way toward a new book of poems when I have accumulated thirteen poems in a stack. One more than a dozen is a slightly extravagant gift of flowers, and it is enough poems for me to believe that I might be able to continue to make them into a book. In a group of thirteen poems, I can identify echoes of sound patterns. Certain related images will show up in more than two poems. Colors or nouns or shapes recur as does conscious or unconscious subject matter. Repetition starts me on assembling a manuscript, and it is this I will attend to most closely at the last stages of putting a book together, as I check for repetitiousness.

These are my rituals, my superstitions. When poets talk about assembling a book of poems, we like to suggest that it is an occult procedure. When asked, poets often insist that the arrangement of a manuscript is too inscrutable—or perhaps unlucky?—to describe in detail. Thinking about how poems are arranged in a collection requires a certain amount of consideration of audience and poets are more reluctant than most artists to talk about how their work might appear to others. "I write for myself and strangers," as Gertrude Stein famously said. Dressing up a book of poems for public consumption may seem to smack of crowd-pleasing, sycophancy, or insufficient attention to the pure call of the inner voice. But the unconscious too, as we know, has its rigid orders. How, then, do we intuit which poems complement each other or which groupings divide into sections? How do we move from one poem to another? How do we recognize which poems keep each other company?

Visual artists seem more willing than poets to talk about the way groups of paintings or sculptures work together in an exhibit. The relationship of one piece to another is an obvious and essential part of the assemblage. While the titles for individual works may not be particularly stimulating ("Red Painting" beside "Blue Painting," or "Potato # 1, # 2, # 3"), the recognition that discrete works of art must interact with each other is manifest. Something serious and obvious would be missing if, for example, "Potato # 3" were removed from the series of eight. Painters often consciously set out to make diptychs or triptychs, which are similar, perhaps, to stanzaic form in poems, but the surface is much larger. A cluster of three paintings on a wall bears more resemblance to three or four poems in a sequence in a book. Similarly, composers and musicians also pay close attention to tempo, mood and register within pieces of music, as well as *among* pieces of music on a single evening's program. The recent increase in the number of poetry books organized in sequences of various kinds suggests that poets have begun to think more about these issues as well. When I talk about the way sequences are assembled, I inevitably start borrowing from the vocabulary of other art forms. In addition to the language of visual art and music, I have found it helpful to borrow from the vocabulary of comics; quilt making; drama and dance as equivalents for putting together clusters or sequences of poems.[1]

As I look around my study at the shelves of poetry books, I can find twenty or thirty recent collections that deal with a single subject matter. I have books about: the West Virginia mine wars, the Triangle Shirtwaist Company Fire, the influenza epidemic of 1918, the Salem witch trials, photographs by E.J. Bellocq of prostitutes in the Storyville district of New Orleans, and the Second World War, the Vietnam War, and the war in Bosnia in 1992-94.[2] In addition, I can find books, or sections of books, that use the biographies of historical or popular culture figures as diverse as Daniel Boone; Annie Oakley; Amelia Earhart; Annie Taylor, the first woman to go over Niagra Falls in a barrel; the dancer, Vaslav Nijinksy; Macnolia Cox, the African-American girl who won the state spelling bee in Ohio in 1936 only to be cheated out of the national title by racist southern judges; Simone Weil; Bob Hope; Cher and Brad Pitt; Billy the Kid; and Emily Carr and Georgia O'Keeffe.[3] I don't know all the reasons for the current interest in books of poems with single subject matter, or books of poems that work in sequences using certain forms. I can speculate however that, as we have come to read history with a twenty-first century skepticism, and as we have come to read fiction in a less linear way than we did in the past, perhaps we are looking to poetry to provide us with a sense of history and of straightforward story telling. All of the books I have noted above are, in some way, *plotted*. Most of them have applied historical research. Their projects are intellectual ones, and the books themselves often have footnotes, or author's notes, epilogues, or introductions that describe in some detail the project's derivation and motivation. Poems in a sequence unified by formal constraints have a similar intellectual genesis and these, too, often provide explanatory information in notes outside the poems themselves.[4]

Groups of poems, of course, usually move sequentially and here, I find it helpful to borrow language from what the comic artist Will Eisner refers to as "the sequential art." We are moved through comic books, or to use the more highfalutin term, graphic novels, by sequenced frames of pictures and words. Like comics, poems move from frame to frame or page to page. In his book *Understanding Comics: The Invisible Art*, Scott McCloud lists six ways comics move from frame to frame: moment to moment; action to action; subject to subject; scene to scene; aspect to aspect; and *non sequitur*.[5]

This, like arrangement by subject matter, is an intellectual approach, calculated for the effects of "linkage and collision" as Muriel Rukeyser has named them.[6] Often, poems are arranged chronologically, moving from moment to moment of a particular event, or following the pattern of the order in which the poet wrote the poems. Especially in poems that chronicle historical events, one action often follows another in the arrangement of the book. Sometimes the order is designed to establish contrast; for example, a battle scene may follow a poem of domestic activity. The perspective on subject matter changes as different voices come into a sequence of poems, and, sometimes, the scene will shift from urban to rural or from interior to exterior. The movement from aspect to aspect, as McCloud defines it, "bypasses time for the most part and sets a wandering eye on a place, idea, or mood."[7] In comics this is established visually; in a book of poems it is usually accomplished by different voices, in different tones and registers, entering into conversation about the same topic. The *non sequitur*, in comics or in poetry, is the surprise, the quick change-up, or the seemingly illogical shift. Many poets use the *non sequitur* in a book of poems as a way of creating tension. It is a way of sustaining interest in poem after poem through the intrigue of the unpredictable.

I use these methods of arrangement when I have a specific project for my stack of thirteen poems. If, after thirteen poems, I can begin to see an obsession emerging – a preoccupation with, for example, vegetables or scat singing or war memorials – then I will follow that lead into the research that may help me find additional organizational patterns for a book. But how does this intellectual patterning lead to the final, largely intuitive stages of arrangement? The art of comics may be a useful heuristic for thinking about the sequencing of poems, but when I consider the contribution of the unconscious to the movement from poem to poem, I think about the making of quilts. Although quilt making uses a very exact, almost mathematical patterning, most quilt makers give themselves permission to break or bend the rules in an effort to make the quilts uniquely their own. The brilliant quilt makers of Gee's Bend, Alabama, almost all of whom were former slaves or descendents of slaves, talk about their search for unique designs in traditional patterns.[8] Beyond their knowledge of traditional patterns (many of which they have collectively redefined), the quilt makers of Gee's Bend use what they have observed in other quilts and their intelligent intuition. It is important to note that intuitive, or unconscious, choices are not mindless ones. Although they do not call upon the rational and cognitive processes of consciousness, they have everything to do with concentrated attention, another way of using our *minds.*

In an interview with Matthew Arnett in March 2002, Gee's Bend quilt maker, Lorraine Pettway describes her process this way:

> How I start to make a quilt, all I do is start sewing, and it just comes to me. My daughter ask me the other day what was I making, and I said, 'I don't know yet; I'm just sewing pieces together,' and the quilt looked pretty good. No pattern, I usually don't use a pattern, *only my mind.* (Emphasis added).[9]

Openly acknowledging the way different art forms may provide useful language for talking about poems, many African-American writers consciously draw on quilt making, as well as on gospel music or the blues, dance patterns, and high-spirited and subversive play in arranging their poems. Poet Harryette Mullen foregrounds this when she discusses her own process in an interview with Barbara Henning:

> My paternal grandmother was an accomplished quilter. The list poems, *Trimmings* and *S*PeRM**K*T,* as well as the stanza form of *Muse and Drudge*, allowed me to make a kind of long poem composed of discreet *(sic)* units, so that in effect, I could write brief, manageable poems that were parts of a longer work that was the book-

> length poem. The discreet units, stanzas or paragraphs, form various patterns like the pieces of a quilt. . . .[10]

Two other processes are helpful to me in making decisions about what to include and what to take out of a book of poems. One is the dramatic, read-everything-out-loud technique. Richard Hugo gives this advice to poets in *The Triggering Town*: "Read your poem aloud many times. If you don't enjoy it every time, something may be wrong." [11] This is good advice for assembling a book of poems as well. Reading the poems aloud over and over and listening to the movement from end line to beginning line, from scene to scene and voice to voice, reveals the book's underlying dramatic structure and helps me to hear more clearly the sound patterns and explicit and inherent forms. At this stage, I often discover poems that I have not written yet. Attention to dramatic parameters makes obvious what is missing. Another way to test this is to plan a poetry reading around a section or two of a book. Hearing the poems with an audience (and hearing yourself reading aloud in the presence of others) can help to identify the dead spots, the points of tension and rest, the arcs of ascent and decline. Harryette Mullen carries this process a step further as she remembers the ways of talking she learned as a young child. She locates her grown-up language games in a way of being among others that she learned very early in her life:

> It was okay to be bookish, but you also had to be able to talk the talk. Playing the dozens, signifying, capping, sounding: all of these forms of verbal dueling were ways we learned to use language, wit, and humor to defend ourselves against verbal aggression. Every child had a large repertoire of formulaic greeting, insults, taunts, and retorts, which often exploited the mnemonic force of rhythm and rhyme.[12]

Another way of arranging a book of poems is through repetition of form. Many poets use repeated formal structures, such as the sonnet, the epistolary form, the journal form, or specific meters such as *terza rima*, heroic couplets, or blank verse. A particularly admirable example of book-length formal pyrotechnics is Marilyn Hacker's book *Love, Death, and the Changing of the Seasons,* which not only tells a fairly straightforward story of a lesbian love affair, but does so in two double-braided crowns of sonnets.

When I assemble a book of poems, usually the very last step I follow is kinetic. I lay all the poems out on the floor and crawl, and then walk, around them. This is the point at which I am likely to discover what could be left out. The kinetic process allows me to feel physically the timing of the poems: which ones are too long, which are too short, and which do not need to be there at all. It alerts me to repetitiousness. The excesses reveal themselves in the kinetic process, as the book begins to take on the shape of a dance. The final stage of a book's arrangement for me is choreographic; I imagine the poems as the outlines of little feet moving forward and backward, sideways and straight ahead, still and in quick motion.

The phrase I took as the title of this essay is one I heard growing up in the mountains of West Virginia. It is a southern idiom and has, like most idiomatic speech, a complex meaning. To "keep company" with someone implies an intimacy that is more than just friendship. It is a relative of serious dating or "going steady." Keeping company requires an exclusivity; some others are shut out. And, of course, it requires selectivity as well. To keep company with someone implies that they have been chosen and that a temporary commitment has been made. The commitment *may* turn out to be permanent – one may keep company and then end up marrying – but permanency is not essential. Keeping company is not a static but a flexible affair, more like an interlude in an evening's program, or a new dance partner.

The poems inside a single collection must keep each other company. They must be chosen from all the poems available at a certain point. Some poems will always end up left on the floor to wait for the next book or eliminated from future consideration. The poems we choose *must* look good together and they must dance well. There may be another, or many other partners in the future, but the poems inside the covers of one book must be intimate and exclusive with each other for a time. They keep company, in a felicitous arrangement of sound, image, color, tone, language, and dramatic tension. They require the resources of the total imagination. When all of this is accomplished, there is a book of poems.

Notes

1. In fall 2005, I taught a graduate course in "The Poetic Sequence" in the consortial MFA program of Northeastern Ohio (NEOMFA). I am grateful to the students in this class for helping me to focus and develop my own ideas about the poetic sequence through their close reading and provocative questions. Thanks to: Evaline Abram-Diroll, Pamela Anderson, Lindsay Bennett, Valerie Suffron Hilty, Anthony Hinckley, Jessica Jewell, Beth Kilbane, Karen Kotrba, Tim McCarthy, Lea Povozhaev, Jill Riga, Jana Russ, Kristen Shuman, Amy Sparks, and Jen Sullivan.
2. The books I refer to are: *Kettle Bottom* by Diane Gilliam Fisher; *Fragments from the Fire: The Triangle Shirtwaist Company Fire of March 25, 1911* by Chris Llewellyn; *Kyrie* by Ellen Bryant Voigt; *The Afflicted Girls* by Nicole Cooley; *Bellocq's Ophelia* by Natasha Trethewey; *Overlord* by Jorie Graham; *The Moon Reflected Fire* by Doug Anderson; and *Rooms and Fields: Dramatic Monologues from the War in Bosnia* by Lee Peterson.
3. The poets I refer to who have written about these figures are: Maurice Manning, Erica Funkhouser, Gabrielle Calvocoressi, Joan Murray, Frank Bidart, A. Van Jordan, Stephanie Strickland, Campbell McGrath, Aaron Smith, Michael Ondaatje, and Kate Braid.
4. Some recent books of poems shaped largely by formal considerations are: *Eve* by Annie Finch; *The Daily Mirror: A Journal in Poetry* by David Lehman; *Sleeping with the Dictionary* by Harryette Mullen; *The Descent of Alette* by Alice Notley; *Darkling* by Anna Rabinowitz; *The Uses of Adversity* by Ron Wallace; and *Jelly Roll (A Blues)* by Kevin Young.
5. Scott McCloud, *Understanding Comics: The Invisible Art* (New York: HarperCollins Publishers, 1993) 70-74.
6. Muriel Rukeyser, *The Life of Poetry* (Ashfield, MA: Paris Press, 1996) 152.
7. McCloud, 72.
8. See: John Beardsley, William Arnett, *et al.*, *The Quilts of Gee's Bend* (Atlanta, GA: Timwood Books in Association with the Museum of Fine Arts, Houston, 2002).

9. Beardsley, 70.
10. Barbara Henning, "An Interview with Harryette Mullen," *The Poetry Project Newsletter* of the Poetry Project of St. Mark's Church, 1996 http://www.poetryproject.com/newsletter/mullen.html.
11. Richard Hugo, *The Triggering Town: Lectures and Essays on Poetry and Writing* (New York: W.W. Norton and Company, Inc., 1979) 39.
12. Henning.

MAGGIE ANDERSON is the author of four books of poems, most recently *Windfall: New and Selected Poems* published in 2000. Her other books include *Cold Comfort* (1986) and *A Space Filled with Moving* (1992). *Maggie Anderson: Greatest Hits 1984-2004* was published in 2004. Anderson is also the editor of the new and selected poems of Louise McNeill and co-editor of *Learning by Heart: Contemporary American Poetry about School* and *A Gathering of Poets*, an anthology of poems to commemorate the 20th anniversary of the shooting of students in an anti-war protest at Kent State University in 1970. Recent poems have been published in *The Alaska Quarterly*, *The Georgia Review*, and *The American Poetry Review*, as well as *Court Green* and *Shenandoah*. Anderson has received fellowships for her poetry from the National Endowment for the Arts and the Ohio Arts Council. In 2004, Anderson was honored as the Appalachian Writer of the Year by Emory and Henry College in Virginia. The 2005 issue of *Iron Mountain Review* is devoted to her work. Maggie Anderson is professor of English and a member of the faculty of the Northeast Ohio MFA program at Kent State University, where she directs the Wick Poetry Center and edits the Wick Poetry Series of the Kent State University Press. She has been honored with the university's Distinguished Teaching Award (2002) and the Distinguished Scholar Award (2004).

PHILIP BRADY's next book of poems, *Fathom*, is forthcoming from Word Press in 2006. His most recent publication is a memoir, *To Prove My Blood: A Tale of Emigrations and the Afterlife* (Ashland Poetry Press). His book of poems, *Weal*, was the 1999 Winner of the Snyder Prize from Ashland University Press, and his first book, *Forged Correspondences* (New Myths), was chosen for Ploughshares Editors' Shelf by Maxine Kumin. He also co-edited, with James F. Carens, *Critical Essays on Portrait of the Artist as a Young Man* (Twayne Publishers). He has won five Ohio Arts Council Individual Artists Awards, a Thayer Fellowship from New York State, and residencies at Yaddo, the Headlands Center for the Arts, the Ragdale Foundation, the Hambidge Center, the Tyrone Guthrie Center in Ireland, Fundacion Valparaiso in Spain, Hawthornden Castle in Scotland, and the Soros Centre for the Arts in the Czech Republic. Brady has taught at the National University of Zaire, University of College Cork in Ireland, and on the faculty of Semester at Sea. Currently, he is Executive Director of Etruscan Press, Poetry Editor for *Artful Dodge*, and guest Poetry Editor for *Provincetown Arts*. He is a Professor of English at

Youngstown State University, where he directs the Poetry Center and plays in the New-Celtic band, Brady's Leap.

WANDA COLEMAN is self-made and self-styled, and regards herself as having matured between two urban uprisings. She was born in the Los Angeles community of Watts, nationally reputed for its August 1965 riot. She was raised in the African-American community of South Central Los Angeles—which rioted in April 1992 following the verdict in the Rodney King beating trial. A Guggenheim fellow, Emmy-winning scriptwriter, and former columnist for *Los Angeles Times* magazine, her work is culled from her perceptions of the conflicts and confusions that shape the cultural terrain of Southern California. She has published over 1100 poems, in over 80 anthologies and periodicals, and is the author of 18 books, including *Ostinato Vamps* (Pitt Poetry Series) and *The Riot Inside Me* (Godine/Black Sparrow Books).

BECKIAN FRITZ GOLDBERG holds an MFA from Vermont College and is the author of several volumes of poetry, *Body Betrayer* (Cleveland State University Poetry Center, 1991), *In the Badlands of Desire* (Cleveland State University Poetry Center, 1993), *Never Be the Horse*, winner of the University of Akron Poetry Prize selected by Thomas Lux (University of Akron Press, 1999), *Twentieth Century Children,* a limited edition chapbook, (Graphic Design Press, Indiana University, 1999), *Lie Awake Lake*, winner of the 2004 Field Poetry Prize (Oberlin College Press, 2005), and *The Book of Accident* (University of Akron Press, forthcoming, 2007.) Her work has appeared widely in anthologies and journals including *The American Poetry Review, The Best American Poetry 1995, Field, The Gettysburg Review, Harper's, Indiana Review, The Iowa Review, New American Poets of the 90's,* and *The Massachusetts Review.* She has been awarded the Theodore Roethke Poetry Prize, The *Gettysburg Review* Annual Poetry Award, the University of Akron Press Poetry Prize, the *Field* Poetry Prize, two Arizona Arts Commission Poetry Fellowships, and a Pushcart Prize. Goldberg currently teaches in the Creative Writing Program at Arizona State University.

SUSAN GRIMM is a native of Cleveland, Ohio. In 1992, she received an MA in English from Cleveland State University. She is a former managing editor of *The Gamut*, Cleveland State University's general interest magazine, and a founding editor of *Ohio Writer*, a service newsletter for writers. She has taught creative writing at Case Western Reserve University and currently teaches poetry at Cleveland State University. She is also the editor for the Cleveland State University Poetry Center. Her poems have appeared in *West Branch, Poetry Northwest, Rattapallax, The Journal*, and other publications. In 1996, she was awarded an Individual Artists Fellowship from the Ohio Arts Council. Her chapbook *Almost Home* was published by the Cleveland State University Poetry Center in 1997. In 1999, she was named Ohio Poet of the Year by the Ohio Poetry Day Association. Her new book of poems, *Lake Erie Blue,* was published by BkMk Press in June of 2004.

JEFF GUNDY's fourth book of poems, *Deerflies,* won the Editions Prize and the 2005 Nancy Dasher Award from the College English Association of Ohio. Earlier books of poems include *Flatlands* (Cleveland State University Poetry Center) and *Rhapsody with Dark Matter* and *Inquiries* (both Bottom Dog Press). His third prose book, *Walker in the Fog: On Mennonite Writing,* was published by Cascadia in 2005. Other recent work is in *The Sun, Shenandoah, Christian Century, North American Review, Georgia Review, Mid-American Review, Artful Dodge,* and *Poet Lore.* He has received five Ohio Arts Council grants in creative writing, taught at the Antioch Writers' Workshop and the Language of Nature Institute, and serves as General Editor for the AWP Intro Awards. Since 1984 he has taught writing, literature, critical theory, American studies, and other classes at Bluffton University.

BONNIE JACOBSON is the author of two poetry collections, *Stopping for Time* (GreenTower Press, Northwest Missouri State University) and *In Joanna's House* (Cleveland State University Poetry Center), and two chapbooks, *On Being Served Apples* (Bits Press, Case Western Reserve University) and *Greatest Hits* (Pudding House). In 1990 she was named Ohio Poet of the Year, and in 1999 was awarded an Ohio Arts Council Individual Artists Fellowship. Her poems have appeared in *The Iowa Review, The Gettysburg Review, Prairie Schooner, Tar River Poetry, Rattle, Runes*, etc., and have been anthologized in *The Bedford Introduction to Literature, The Random House Treasury of Light Verse, I Have My Own Song For It* (The University Of Akron Press) and *O Taste and See* and *Family Matters* (Bottom Dog Press). Most recently, she edited the Poets' & Writers' League of Greater Cleveland's popular anthology, *Cleveland in Prose and Poetry,* which she arranged in five historical sections.

Author Biographies

KAREN KOVACIK is Director of Creative Writing at Indiana University Purdue University Indianapolis. She's the author of the poetry collections *Metropolis Burning* (Cleveland State University Poetry Center, 2005), *Beyond the Velvet Curtain* (Kent State, 1999), and *Nixon and I* (Kent State, 1998). The recipient of a 2004-2005 Fulbright grant to Poland, she has published translations of contemporary Polish poets in *American Poetry Review*, *Crazyhorse*, *West Branch*, and *The Lyric*. She has received awards from the University of Wisconsin's Institute for Creative Writing, the Ohio Arts Council, and the Arts Council of Indianapolis.

ROBERT MILTNER is the author of seven chapbooks, including the Wick Award-winning *Against the Simple*, and recently *Rock the Boat* (All Nations Press) and *Canyons of Sleep* (Plan B Press); three limited edition/artists' books, including *Ghost of a Chance* (Zygote Press) and *Northcoast, Ohio* (Spare Change Press); and *Marc Snyder: In Black and White* (Kent State University Stark), an art exhibition catalog. He teaches literature, composition, and creative writing at Kent State University Stark where he directs the Enormous Room Reading Series. His essays on Terry Tempest Williams, Virginia Woolf, James Joyce, J.D. Salinger, Rane Arroyo and Raymond Carver have been published in the US, Puerto Rico, India, and the UK, and his poems, reviews, and stories have appeared in journals such as *Artful Dodge, Barrow Street, CrossConnect, Diagram, Hawai'i Pacific Review, Mid-American Review, Pleiades, Prose Poem, Sentence, Sleeping Fish, Vincent Brothers Review, Vox,* and *Wisconsin Review.* Miltner holds a BA from Xavier University of Ohio, an MEd from John Carroll University, and a PhD from Kent State University. He is the editor for the forthcoming *Raymond Carver Review*.

LIZ ROSENBERG is the author of three books of poems, five anthologies of poetry for young readers, and two novels. Her newest book, *The Purpose of Beauty*, is due out in 2006-2007 from Mammoth Press, to be followed by *The Foundling* from Curbstone. She teaches English and Creative Writing at the State University of New York at Binghamton and has published poems in *The New Yorker*, *Harper's*, *Poetry*, *The American Poetry Review*, and *Best American Poems 2006*, selected by Billy Collins.

AMY BRACKEN SPARKS is an award-winning critic, writer, and poet. Former arts editor for the *Cleveland Free Times*, she won top honors in film criticism from the Association of Alternative Newspapers in 1995, Best Critic in Ohio in 1998, and Best Columnist in Ohio in 2000 from the Society of Professional Journalists, as well as numerous other local press awards. She is the author of two books of poetry, *serious red* (Cleveland State University Poetry Center, 1996) and *queen of cups* (Burning Press, 1993), and has had work published in *American Poetry Review, Denver Quarterly, Southern Poetry Review, Nimrod, ArtCrimes, Mirage Period(ical), Kiosk, situation*, and *Whiskey Island*. An essay, "Strike," was included in the anthology *In Buckeye Country* (Bottom Dog Press, 1994). She is the recipient of two Ohio Arts Council Individual Fellowships for media arts and poetry, as well as a residency at Headlands Center for the Arts in San Francisco. She was also co-founder and co-director of the sound art and new music festival, Sonic Disturbance.

CAROLYNE WRIGHT has published eight books and chapbooks of poetry, three collections of poetry in translation from Spanish and Bengali, and a collection of essays. Her Blue Lynx Prize and American Book Award-winning book, *Seasons of Mangoes and Brainfire*, appeared in a second edition from Eastern Washington UP/Lynx House Books in 2005. Her new collection is *A Change of Maps* (Lost Horse Press, 2006). Forthcoming is *Majestic Nights: Love Poems of Bengali Women* (White Pine, 2007). Wright's investigative memoir in progress of her experiences in Chile on a Fulbright Study Grant during the presidency of Salvador Allende, *The Road to Isla Negra*, received the PEN/Jerard Fund and the Crossing Boundaries Awards. She spent four years on Indo-U.S. Subcommission and Fulbright Senior Research fellowships in India and Bangladesh, translating the work of Bengali women poets and writers. Wright has received several awards from the Poetry Society of America and *Nimrod* Magazine (Pablo Neruda Prize); fellowships from the Seattle Arts Commission, Witter Bynner Foundation, NEA, and New York State Council on the Arts; she has been a Writing Fellow at the Fine Arts Work Center in Provincetown, Vermont Studio Center, and Yaddo. A visiting professor at colleges, universities, and writers' conferences around the country, including Cleveland State University in 2004-2005, Wright recently moved back to her native Seattle, and currently teaches in the Whidbey Writers Workshop MFA Program. She is Translation Editor for *Artful Dodge*, and on the Board of Directors of the AWP for 2004-2008.